More than Swings and Roundabouts

Planning for outdoor play

Children's Play Council

NATIONAL
CHILDREN'S
BUREAU

making a difference

The **Children's Play Council** aims to raise awareness of the importance of play in children's lives and the need for all children to have access to better play opportunities and play services.

Set up in 1988, CPC is an alliance of national and regional organisations and local authorities. Its work reaches wherever children play: at home, in play areas, parks, school playgrounds and streets, in play and childcare centres, in hospitals and community health settings, in cities and in the countryside.

The **National Children's Bureau** promotes the interests and well-being of all children and young people across every aspect of their lives. NCB advocates the participation of children and young people in all matters affecting them. NCB challenges disadvantage in childhood.

NCB achieves its mission by
- ensuring the views of children and young people are listened to and taken into account at all times
- playing an active role in policy development and advocacy
- undertaking high quality research and work from an evidence-based perspective
- promoting multidisciplinary, cross-agency partnerships
- identifying, developing and promoting good practice
- disseminating information to professionals, policy makers, parents and children and young people.

NCB has adopted and works within the UN Convention on the Rights of the Child.

Published by National Children's Bureau Enterprises Ltd, the trading company for the National Children's Bureau, Registered Charity number 258825. 8 Wakley Street, London EC1V 7QE. Tel: 020 7843 6000

© National Children's Bureau, 2002
Published 2002

ISBN 1 900990 74 1

British Library Cataloguing in Publication Data
A catalogue record for this book is available from the British Library

Typeset by Jeff Teader
Cover designed by Sharon Casteldine
Printed and bound by ColourBooks Ltd, Dublin

CONTENTS

ACKNOWLEDGEMENTS

This guide was compiled and written by Issy Cole-Hamilton and Tim Gill of the Children's Play Council. It is based on information, advice and support supplied by many people. These include:

An Advisory Group: Alan Barber (Institute of Leisure and Amenity Management), Helen Crofts (Department for Local Government, Transport and the Regions), Phil Doyle (Play in the Community, Hounslow), Caroline Field (Moat Housing Society), Yvonne Gilligan (Groundwork UK), Jackie Hall (National Society for the Prevention of Cruelty to Children), Tim Head (Portsmouth County Council), Debbie Lye (Department for Culture, Media and Sport), Chris Martin (Devon@Play), Peter Matthew (Department for Local Government, Transport and the Regions), Sandra Melville (PLAYLINK), Joanna Ryam (Kidsactive), Jean Wenger (National Playing Fields Association), Rob Wheway (Institute of Leisure and Amenity Management)

Play providers and staff from Groundwork Trusts in the West Midlands: Dave Boucker (Evesham Adventure Playground), Carolyn Granthier (Groundwork West Durham), Nick Illingworth (Groundwork Dearne Valley), Helen Johnson (Groundwork Erewash Valley), Roy Mosley (Groundwork Creswell), Keith Rimmer (Walsall MBC), Jo Webb (Groundwork Birmingham)

Leeds City Council Green Spaces Planning Group

Project managers involved in developing innovative and interesting practice (see Contacts for case studies, page 99)

Children's Play Council and National Children's Bureau staff: Sharon Castledine (designer), Sabina Collier, Mark Dunn, Pennie Hedge, Bethany Rawles

Children and young people from across England who gave their time and their views in local consultations reviewed by the Children's Play Council, 2002. Quotes from these consultations appear throughout the guide

The guide is funded by the Department for Local Government, Transport and the Regions, Groundwork UK (through the Barclays SiteSaver Programme), Garfield Weston Foundation and Sutcliffe Play.

INTRODUCTION

'I made my escape as soon as I could and slipped down to the river to find the old hiding place. The wilderness was gone, the tree had been felled and a neat summer house had been erected "to please the children"'
TS Eliot, The Family Reunion

'Too many young people these days are treated as an environmental problem, to be swept off the streets like litter. Groundwork's experience over the last twenty years shows that, given the right support and skills, young people can be a powerful and positive force for improving the quality of community life.'
*Tony Hawkhead,
Groundwork Chief Executive*

This guide argues for a new approach to creating and improving opportunities for outdoor play and informal recreation for children and young people. Instead of starting with spaces – playgrounds, parks, playing fields – we need to start with children and young people and their needs, wishes and entitlements. We need to look at, and perhaps change, our values, principles and understandings about children, play and free time. Crucially, we need to acknowledge that children and young people are legitimate users of the whole of the outdoor environment. Therefore, this book proposes some key principles, techniques and approaches and gives sources of detailed information and support.

Trends in land use and planning over much of the post-war period have left children and young people with less access to public open space, focusing instead on priorities such as meeting the needs of ever-increasing volumes of motor traffic. Where planners and managers have addressed outdoor spaces, they have tended to neglect local circumstances, too often relying on cost-saving measures and 'off the shelf' solutions. However, growing concerns about children's and young people's free time and a revived interest in the built environment, especially in urban areas, are opening up a range of partnership initiatives and funding streams. These, in turn, are creating new opportunities to improve outdoor play and informal recreation for children and young people.

Children and young people have always spent much of their time out of doors – in parks, playgrounds, streets and other open spaces. Few people would disagree with the view that this is healthy and right – for them, their families and the wider community. And in spite of growing restrictions on their mobility, large numbers of children and young people are still spending time outside their homes, and many more would like to do so. But whereas a generation ago little public attention was given to children's and young people's use of the outdoor environment, today their needs, their wishes, their activities and indeed their very presence out of doors is the source of major concern and debate.

By making sure all children and young people have access to good outdoor space, we as a society will be:
■ responding to their stated needs and wishes;
■ supporting their healthy physical, social and emotional development;
■ contributing to a reduction in their feelings of exclusion;
■ contributing to the promotion of safer, more harmonious and more cohesive communities.
If we do not offer children and young people good access to attractive, engaging outdoor spaces where they can enjoy themselves, we should not be surprised if they seek out other, more problematic places and activities.

Central Government determines the framework for local planning, through both legislation and guidance. Key planning guidance affecting children's and young people's outdoor play space includes Planning Policy Guidance Notes: PPG3, relating to housing development; and PPG17, relating to outdoor space for play, recreation and sport (DETR, 2000a; DTLR, 2002).

Recent changes in local planning systems, which require community participation and better integrated planning within local authorities, offer local authorities new opportunities to plan for children's outdoor play within the context of local neighbourhood and community needs.

In some parts of the country in the next 10 years or more, there will be large-scale house building and new development, offering a good opportunity to include children's and young people's outdoor play space as an integral design element. In other areas existing land is being redeveloped and its use changed. The impact of redevelopment of outdoor space and facilities can have a major impact on children and young people, positively or negatively.

However, most children and young people live in areas where major redevelopment or alterations to the built environment are unlikely. But here, even modest changes can make a real difference to their access to and use of outdoor space.

Who this guide is for?

This guide is for all those involved in maintaining and developing public open spaces in or near residential areas, in both urban and rural settings. It is also for residents and workers who wish to get involved in creating or improving places where children and young people can play and spend their free time.

This guide is for:
- local authority personnel: landscape architects, parks and leisure managers, planners, highways and transport professionals, designers, housing managers, senior managers and elected members;
- town and parish councils;
- people involved in providing outdoor space including regeneration partnerships, developers, housing associations and voluntary sector providers.

It will also be of use to:
- policy makers involved in local planning and strategic development, housing, public open space, traffic and transport, rural issues, children's health and well-being, community safety, children's and young people's leisure and cultural needs, social exclusion and equality issues;

- play service managers and play development officers.
- parents, community activists, children and young people, community development workers, play service staff, staff working locally to develop play space.

This guide is particularly relevant where there is an existing local population. However, many of the principles (such as the need to plan across a whole neighbourhood and to consider location and access issues) are also relevant to new developments. Even the sections on participation may have relevance if developer agencies are able to make preliminary contact with new residents, or alternatively to defer work on some aspects of the development (as happens, for instance, in the Netherlands).

The guide puts into context, but does not repeat, other recent works about the technical design and safety of children's and young people's outdoor play spaces, some of which are listed in Appendix 1. Although written with an English readership in mind, many of the issues are similar in Wales, Scotland and Northern Ireland.

Whether you are planning to refurbish or develop a small neighbourhood play area, or improve outdoor play space throughout a neighbourhood, the process and principles remain the same. This simple checklist should help you ensure you are making the most of the resources available to you in developing effective, sustainable outdoor play space. It will also help you navigate through the rest of this guide.

Getting started (Chapter 2)

Are you involving the right people?

These include:

1 Local authority departments, officers and members whose decisions and actions might affect the outdoor play space, including those with responsibility for:
✓ developing community strategies, a statutory requirement for local authorities;
✓ developing cultural strategies and services;
✓ supporting regeneration and renewal;
✓ youth and educational provision;
✓ tackling social exclusion;
✓ granting permission for new residential developments;
✓ planning and developing residential areas;
✓ developing town or parish plans;
✓ ensuring quality social housing;
✓ promoting community safety and harmony;
✓ managing highways, traffic and transport;
✓ maintaining 'open spaces';
✓ providing dedicated services for children and young people.

2 Partnerships and initiatives that may have an interest in developing outdoor play space, including:
✓ Local Strategic Partnerships;
✓ Early Years Development and Childcare Partnerships (EYDCPs);
✓ Community Safety Partnerships;
✓ Neighbourhood Renewal Partnerships;
✓ Children's Fund and Sure Start Partnerships.

3 Voluntary sector and other local organisations with an interest in services for children and young people and open spaces.

Are all those involved working together to agreed values and principles?

Are you involving children and young people and getting maximum benefit from their involvement?

You can achieve this by:
✓ employing methods appropriate to the situation;
✓ ensuring the adults involved have the right skills and attitudes to children and young people;
✓ recognising and using the basic principles for any participative work;
✓ involving children and young people at the outset or in the early stages of planning;
✓ giving targeted attention to some groups where needed.

Are you developing clearly stated SMART objectives?

✓ **Specific:** clearly defined and easy to understand.
✓ **Measurable:** so you know whether or not you are successful.
✓ **Achievable:** within the timescale you anticipate.
✓ **Resourced:** achievable within the resources available.
✓ **Timed:** with a clear and realistic timetable.

Are you identifying and addressing potential barriers to success?

These include:
✓ concerns about potential safety issues;
✓ difficulties with insurance cover;
✓ conflict between different groups;
✓ problems over land use.

How do you intend to establish exactly what needs to be done?

1 You will need to carry out an outdoor play audit to find out about:
✓ children and young people in the locality – who they are, where they play and why they play in those places;
✓ existing plans for the development of local spaces;
✓ costs, funding and other resources involved.

2 You will need to compare the supply of and demand for play space, in order to:
✓ identify where needs of different groups are currently being met and not being met;
✓ establish 'what works' now;
✓ identify problems with existing provision.

Are you identifying both capital and revenue funding if necessary?

Making changes (Chapter 3)

Are you ensuring that the space/s you are developing follow the general principles for sustainable outdoor play spaces?

Check they are:
✓ going to actively attract children and young people;
✓ located in sites which are:
  • reasonably close to home
  • within sight of main travel routes
  • in spaces where there is 'informal oversight'
✓ easily accessible and usable by children who are disabled as well as those who are non-disabled;
✓ felt to offer personal security;
✓ accessible to all who may wish to use them;
✓ flexible enough to allow for changing play fashions, interests and needs;
✓ frequently cleaned and well maintained.

Do the spaces you are developing follow the essential design principles of a good play environment?

These include:
✓ both simple and complex environments to play in;
✓ play opportunities accessible to all those who might want to use them, in line with the Disability Discrimination Act 1995;
✓ creative and stimulating environments.

Have you considered all the possible types of dedicated play space you might provide, bearing in mind the ages and interests of the different groups of children and young people?

These include:
✓ playgrounds;
✓ skateboard and skate parks;
✓ bike tracks and jumps;
✓ hangout or youth shelters;
✓ adventure playgrounds;
✓ other open access play projects;
✓ city farms, woodland spaces and nature reserves;
✓ multi-use games areas;
✓ fun trails and activity courses;
✓ school playgrounds.

Are you looking at ways of improving other places where children and young people play?

These include:
✓ parks, green spaces and commons;
✓ residential streets;
✓ other open spaces.

Key points in this chapter:

- Play is about children and young people having control over their time.
- Good outdoor play opportunities also help families and communities.
- Children and young people make use of the whole of the outdoor environment.
- Some children and young people may need persuading of the pleasures and benefits of outdoor play.
- Children and young people's use of the outdoors has become increasingly restricted.
- 'Quick-fix' solutions may not work.

Play is about children and young people having control over their time

'I'd walk home on my own, drop all my stuff off and go wherever I want with my friends; play in the park and go back to my house. I don't like adults with me as bigger boys think it's silly.'

'Play' is what children and young people do when not being directed by adults. It is a natural part of their daily life and healthy development. Children and young people of all ages play. The word 'play' may not always sound appropriate, and as children get older the words they and adults use to describe their activities change, perhaps using terms for specific activities. For simplicity the term 'play' is used throughout this guide.

Play is different from other activities in that it is entirely directed and controlled by the child or young person and has no adult-driven agenda. The essence of play is that children and young people choose what they will do, how they will do it and with whom, when they will start and stop and what the outcome, if any, will be. Rules and boundaries are invented and negotiated by the children and young people, and all decisions relevant to the activity are made by those playing.

Best Play, a key document from the play sector, defines play as 'freely chosen, personally directed, intrinsically motivated behaviour that actively engages the child'. The definition draws on values, principles and understandings from the playwork profession (NPFA and others, 2000). *Best Play* puts forward seven objectives that state what play provision should be aiming to do for children and young people:

1 Extend the choice and control that children have over their play, the freedom they enjoy and the satisfaction they gain from it.
2 Recognise the child's need to test boundaries, and respond positively to that need.
3 Manage the balance between the need to offer risk and the need to keep children safe from harm.
4 Maximise the range of play opportunities.
5 Foster independence and self-esteem.
6 Foster children's respect for others and offer opportunities for social interaction.
7 Foster the child's well-being, healthy growth and development, knowledge and understanding, creativity and capacity to learn.

'The right to play is a child's first claim on the community. No community can infringe that right without doing deep and enduring harm to the minds and bodies of its citizens.'
David Lloyd George

Article 31 of the UN Convention on the Rights of the Child confers on every child and young person up to 18 years old the right to 'engage in play and recreational activities appropriate to the age of the child'. Outdoor play is an important element in the realisation of this right.

Children and young people enjoy playing outdoors and it is good for them

'When I go out it gets air to my brain so that I can think and stuff.'

Children and young people often play outdoors. Even with the range of indoor leisure activities available in their homes and in other places, they still want to spend time in outdoor spaces. Moreover, large numbers children and young people feel they do not have enough opportunities to spend time out of doors.

The single strongest message from children and young people about their play and free time is that they want to spend more time outside, according to a research review in 2001/2 of over 100 local consultations from across England. The research, undertaken by the Children's Play Council, included Early Years Development and Childcare Plan audits, Best Value reviews, Children's Fund and Health Action Zone consultations and covered a total of over 14,000 children and young people, nearly all aged 5–16 (Cole-Hamilton and others, 2002).

In a survey in Northamptonshire nearly 75 per cent of the 9- to 16-year- old young people questioned described themselves as 'outdoor people' rather than 'indoor people' and more than 80 per cent said they preferred being out and about than staying in (Matthews and others, 1998).

Outdoor play opens up a whole range of enjoyable activities alone and with friends. It often involves healthy physical activity, so it plays a part in reducing the long-term health consequences of a sedentary lifestyle. It is important as a way of learning key social, emotional and life skills. The more diverse the natural and physical surroundings, the greater the range of possible experiences and learning and developmental opportunities.

Playing outdoors gives children and young people a whole range of play opportunities not otherwise available to them. Outside they are more able to play freely, meet their friends, move around on foot or by bicycle, feel less constrained in their activities, to run, climb, jump and hide. They have the chance to learn about and to feel a sense of ownership of the local environment. For older young people outdoor space offers them a place, away from the gaze and demands of adults, where they can meet their friends, socialise with people of their own age and develop their own sense of identity.

Children playing outdoors are certain to encounter potential difficulties and challenges – physical, emotional, mental and social. As they do so they learn from adults, their friends and through experience, how to look after themselves and how to react and behave in different situations. Learning to confront difficult situations and test boundaries is a normal and important part of growing up, which is denied to children who are never in a position where they have to deal with difficulties.

A Government-funded study in Zurich in the mid-1990s suggested that five-year-old children who were not in the habit of playing outside their homes with their friends because their parents thought it was too dangerous were restricted in their social relationships, made fewer friends when they started school, were less able to occupy themselves and were more likely to watch television in their 'free time' than children who played out on the street near their homes (Huttenmoser and Degen-Zimmerman, 1995).

Good outdoor play opportunities also help families and communities

Understanding the outdoor play needs of children and young people can lead to better provision for everyone and more harmonious community relations. Where children and young people have a range of attractive outdoor play spaces and activities available to them in accessible, safe locations, and are fully engaged in activities they enjoy, they are less likely to encroach on the space and sensibilities of adults. Parents will be reassured that their children can enjoy positive activities out of doors, and there is likely to be less conflict with other local residents. The spaces themselves and the process of creating and improving them may also contribute to building social cohesion and supporting informal networks of family support, bringing communities together and adding to the 'social capital' of a neighbourhood.

Community-based evaluations show that projects lead to improvements in connections and trust in the local community. 'Prove it!', an approach to evaluation developed by the New Economics Foundation, Barclays plc and Groundwork UK, has been piloted in outdoor play and recreation spaces and showed a measurable impact on local interaction, new friendships, community know-how and community safety (New Economics Foundation, 2001).

The Swiss study quoted above suggested that the parents of the five-year-olds also benefited if they lived in areas that allowed their children good access to outdoor play. For instance, they were more likely to know their neighbours and to be able to arrange informal childcare (Huttenmoser and Degen-Zimmerman, 1995).

Children and young people make use of the whole of the outdoor environment

Given the chance, children and young people spend time in a wide range of outdoor spaces. They also want to get to and from these places confidently on their own; indeed, for many children and young people moving from place to place is half the fun, and research shows that in well-designed neighbourhoods they spend more time on the move than in any one place.

For many children the primary outdoor play spaces are the streets and other open spaces near their homes. Nevertheless, in most areas there is some form of dedicated play provision, for example, unsupervised play spaces such as playgrounds, cycling and skateboard tracks, youth shelters and kick-about areas and, in some areas, staffed open access play provision such as adventure playgrounds and play-schemes.

Parks and other green spaces are often popular with adults taking young children out to play and with young people wanting to spend time together relatively undisturbed.

Some children and young people may need persuading of the pleasures and benefits of outdoor play

Some children and young people rarely play outdoors and may be missing out on important opportunities for physical exercise and social interaction. For them, outdoor play opportunities need to feel safe and be an attractive alternative to their home entertainment. Children and young people are more likely to play outdoors if they and their parents feel they are safe, if there are interesting things for them to do, if their choice of activities is not too restricted and if there are places they can meet with their friends.

It is widely held that school-age children are not particularly interested in outdoor play, preferring instead to stay indoors watching television and playing on computers. Surveys of children's views suggest that, in general, this is an inaccurate picture of their interests. However, where it is true of particular groups of children, there are likely to be two main reasons.

- When children are young, busy parents or carers frequently do not have the time or energy to take them out to play. At the age when they would most naturally be starting to go out and play on their own or with their friends many children have had little experience of outdoor play and their indoor play habits are well established.
- For those who have been taken out to play by their parents or carers, many have only visited parks and playgrounds, often designed with younger children in mind, and may not be aware of the other possibilities for them. They have also always been accompanied and closely supervised by adults and may not feel

safe or comfortable going out on their own. Working parents may also feel more at ease if their children are at home rather than out on the streets.

Children and young people's use of the outdoors has become increasingly restricted

Recent studies in both urban and rural areas indicate that children's and young people's use of the outdoors has become increasingly restricted in the last 20–30 years. More and faster traffic, more parents driving children to school, greater security on private land, declining standards in playground maintenance and real and perceived dangers from other people (children as well as adults) have all combined to reduce children's outdoor play activities.

In his description of growing up in Parkeston, an English village in the 1950s, Tovell describes the fun the children had in their surroundings. They played in the woods building camps, leapt on to the Tarzan swing 'flying through the air and landing flat on your back in the mud at the bottom with the wind knocked out of you'. They slid down the local hill on cardboard and tin in the summer and sledges in the winter. They played in the 'Brickfield' crawling though tunnels only just big enough for them (Tovell, 2000).

But children in Parkeston today have fewer opportunities to play out than Tovell and his friends in the 1950s. Most of their exciting places to play have disappeared and the home life offers more for children. They often have their own bedrooms, television, radios and sound systems. There are also fewer children around to play with as the demography of the village changes. Parents work away from the village and see less of their neighbours. They do not get to know their children's friends and so feel more threatened by the local young people who are strangers to them. The roads are also more dangerous because there is so much more traffic (Tovell, 2000).

In 1997 research found that the parents of children in rural England were so concerned for their children's safety that they heavily supervised their children's use of space. Children's free play and independent environmental exploration was constrained as their parents acted as chauffeurs for them and their friends, taking them to organised activities. Free play in the countryside was also restricted by changes in farming practices (Valentine, 1997).

Other research into the use of urban parks has found that although many adults considered parks to be good places for children, they were concerned that the parks they knew might not be safe or properly maintained. Many were unhappy about their children going to parks on their own. Children were aware of their parents' fears and frequently stayed indoors unless accompanied out by an adult or an older child (Greenhalgh and Worpole, 1995).

Factors that restrict children's and young people's outdoor play

Safety concerns
- anxieties about personal safety, particularly the fear of strangers;
- traffic dangers;
- fear of street crime and bullying.

Poor spaces
- closure of run-down playgrounds;
- poorly maintained playgrounds;
- inappropriate or boring playground design;
- a lack of skilled, 'people oriented' staff in parks;
- play areas located in places that do not feel safe or are hard to get to.

Public policies and planning practices
- the sale of outdoor spaces for development, especially in some urban areas;
- new social housing developments, which tend to favour small individual gardens and less communal open space;
- new buildings and roads in what were previously urban open spaces;
- reductions in play and youth services.

Public attitudes to children and young people
- complaints from adults.

Broader social changes
- more fragmented communities;
- the growth of indoor entertainment and warmer, larger homes;
- changes in farming practices in rural areas.

Any consideration of outdoor play must address the attention given to the threat from strangers. However, it is important to keep this threat in perspective. The numbers of children and young people harmed by adults they do not know is extremely low, and the growth in fear in recent years is not based on any increase in the real risks children face. That said, parents' and children's concerns may need to be addressed. In some spaces, increased supervision may be appropriate. But in many, general improvements that result in increased use will generate a feeling of 'safety in numbers', and hence reduce the level of fear.

There are times when adults intervene to set boundaries on the activities of children and young people playing. Children learn through the reactions and guidance of other children and of adults they respect. If a child does not respect an adult they are less likely to take any notice of what is said, and advice and restrictions imposed on them are likely to be ignored.

'Quick-fix' solutions may not work

'No things for teenagers to do after school – there is nowhere to go, you just hang around the streets.'
A 14-year-old female

Improving children's and young people's access to outdoor play is not always easy. Play has in the past been seen to be less important than other publicly funded services. In many areas it still tends not to be a priority and is often poorly resourced. Many 'solutions' may have short-term benefits but can create long-term problems. In some areas, even where money and resources have been put into initiatives, they have not always been successful.

All too often children's outdoor play space provision fails because solutions attempt to address the immediate problems and not the underlying reasons. For example, merely replacing play equipment that has been vandalised, without looking at why the vandalism took place, makes it very likely that the new equipment will also be vandalised.

Planning play space needs to be clearly thought out. Some 'quick-fix' solutions may cause long-term problems

Short-term solution	Long-term problem
A run-down playground is closed because this is cheaper than repairing it, or extra houses are built on what could otherwise be communal space	Children and young people with nowhere to play can become bored, unfit and possibly play in places where they may be a danger to themselves or a nuisance to others.
Regular cleaning of play areas is cut because it is not seen as 'cost effective'.	Children and young people learn that their spaces are not valued, and that keeping the environment clean and well kept is not important.
New fixed equipment is installed in a poorly used play space, rather than exploring the reasons for poor use.	Children continue to ignore the play space and play elsewhere, possibly in more dangerous places or in places that lead to conflict with others. Children and young people see money being wasted while their needs are not being met.

Children and young people are banned from some areas to pacify complaining residents.	Children and young people become frustrated when their wishes are ignored. They learn that their activities are not wanted, and that the loudest complainant wins in a conflict.
A new housing development caters only for young children on the assumption that families will move away as their children grow up.	Children and young people in families who stay in the area have no facilities and can cause problems for others.
Security staff in cars are employed to patrol a park because it is cheaper than employing skilled park rangers.	Children and young people see the parks as a hostile place and may be less likely to use it.

2.1 Involving the right people

Key points in this section:

- Within local authorities key professionals across many departments should be involved
- Some key partnerships and initiatives should also be involved
- In some areas voluntary sector and other local organisations are important providers
- Multi-disciplinary working supports effective planning and delivery
- Parents and other local residents need to be involved
- All those involved need to agree shared values and principles

Within local authorities, key professionals across many departments should be involved

A Government-endorsed guide to play and cultural strategies states that:
It is important that local authorities avoid the temptation to bracket off children's play into one or more forms of provision, or to represent play simply through a parks or playground service-based approach…The streets, canals and riversides, parks and open spaces – as distinct from designated playgrounds – are places where children must be seen, heard and given opportunities to play
PLAYLINK, 2002

Local authorities have traditionally been the custodians of public open spaces and still have a lead role in developing and protecting these spaces, sometimes as members of a partnership. In some areas town and parish councils also have a key role. It is not unusual for outdoor play to be seen as the sole responsibility of a leisure or parks department. However, given that children and young people frequently play in the streets near their homes, in public parks and other green spaces and in a wide variety of other local open spaces, as well as in dedicated play and youth provision, the activities of most local authority sections will impact in some way on children's and young people's use of the outdoors.

The outdoor play space needs of children and young people should be the concern of those involved in:
- developing community strategies, a statutory requirement for local authorities;
- developing cultural strategies and services;
- supporting regeneration and renewal;
- youth and educational provision;
- tackling social exclusion;
- granting permission for new residential developments;
- planning and developing residential areas;
- developing town or parish plans;
- ensuring quality social housing;
- promoting community safety and harmony;
- managing highways, traffic and transport;
- maintaining 'open spaces';
- providing dedicated services for children and young people.

Most local authority leisure departments have a named person responsible for dedicated outdoor play provision. In some areas there may also be a play development officer. Landscape architects are increasingly working with children, young people and other members of the community to help develop their skills and knowledge about outdoor play.

Potential areas of involvement by different local government departments

Area of local authority	Potential involvement
Community strategy development	These overarching strategies need to address children's and young people's quality of life, in which play has a key role.
Planning and regeneration	All changes to the built environment and public spaces impact on children's and young people's use of those spaces.
Housing development	In many areas those responsible for housing development are the main providers of children's outdoor play space.
Social housing planning, management and maintenance	Social housing tends to have a higher child population, fewer opportunities to use commercial facilities and poorer public space provision.
Highways and transport planning	Many streets are still widely used for play, apart from their significance in trips to friends, play spaces and leisure facilities.
Street maintenance	Street lighting, crossings, pavements and dedicated foot and cycle paths need to be provided and in good working order.
Road safety	Road safety teams have a key role in making it safer for children and young people to use and get around their streets.
Parks and open spaces	Changes in the use or management of these areas can have a major impact on outdoor play space.
Leisure and cultural services	Government guidance (DCMS, 2000) advises that children's play be addressed in the development of local cultural strategies.

Potential areas of involvement by different local government departments (cont.)

Play services	Where they exist local play service managers have a development and coordination role, and may take the lead in developing corporate play policies and strategies. In the absence of play officers, it is often parks staff with no access to play expertise who are responsible for the provision of play facilities.
Environmental protection and implementation of local Agenda 21	Children can benefit from both participation and environmental projects which result in better places for them to play.
Landscape architects	The design and landscaping of public open spaces can determine the potential play value of the space.
Education and schools	Schools are increasingly being encouraged to open their facilities to local communities for wider use and to local children as places for free-time play and activities.
Public health	Professionals concerned about child health can be important champions for the development and protection of outdoor play spaces.
Youth services	In many areas, as children get older, meeting their needs, including their needs for outdoor space and activities, becomes the duty of dedicated youth services.
Legal and health and safety departments	Fear of litigation by parents of children hurt in playground accidents is cited as one of the main reasons for reducing play provision. The approach of the legal department to legal issues has a major impact on outdoor play opportunities.
Equal opportunities sections	Groups of children from social minorities, for example, those who are disabled, have not always had

Potential areas of involvement by different local government departments (cont.)

	the same opportunities to play outdoors as others. Implementation of the Disability Discrimination Act 1995 applies to outdoor play spaces and may require specialist advice and support. There may also be differences in the way children from different ethnic or cultural groups use outdoor space, or in their access to the outdoors.
Community development teams	Regeneration increasingly involves community development approaches, and staff need to be able to engage with and understand the needs of local children and young people.
Social work teams	Two of the Quality Protects priority objectives for 2002/3 are to improve the life chances of children in public care through expenditure on more and better opportunities to participate in leisure, the creative arts and sporting activities, and to target expenditure towards better integration of disabled children into mainstream leisure and free time activities. Outdoor play opportunities are a key part of this.
Child protection teams	Child protection teams may inform consultation and participation processes, and may be involved in the employment of some key staff, for example those in parks and playgrounds.
Local authority voluntary sector grant programmes	In many areas, voluntary sector play projects are funded through programmes managed by officers based in voluntary sector liaison teams. These officers, and the elected politicians they report to, are important in ensuring the continuity and effectiveness of the services being provided.

Some key partnerships should also be involved in developing outdoor play space

Local planning and development is increasingly coordinated by partnerships. Those likely to have an interest in promoting and developing outdoor play include:

- Local Strategic Partnerships;
- Early Years Development and Childcare Partnerships (EYDCPs);
- Community Safety Partnerships;
- Neighbourhood Renewal Partnerships;
- Children's Fund and Sure Start Partnerships.

Local Strategic Partnerships

Local Strategic Partnerships are new bodies, designed to achieve greater joined-up working in a local area. They are developing a wide range of functions, many of which impact on children and young people's outdoor play space. They will prepare and implement local community strategies; identify and respond to priority needs; coordinate local plans, partnerships and initiatives to ensure public service providers work effectively to meet local needs and priorities; support the development of public service agreements (PSAs) which meet suitable targets; and develop and deliver local neighbourhood renewal strategies which secure more jobs, better education, improved health, reduced crime and better housing.

Child on a swing in North Hulme Adventure Playground
Photo by Manchester Adventure Play

Manchester: adventure playgrounds are integral to urban regeneration

Of the six Single Regeneration Budget (SRB) areas in Manchester, four have included adventure playground developments, or aim to do so.

One of these areas is Wythenshawe, an area of major unemployment, unmodernised housing, poor health, relatively high crime and low educational attainment, where there are several major initiatives under way to create a renewed vibrant and prosperous area of the city. The development of Benchill Adventure Playground contributed to these initiatives. It is being redeveloped as its current location on the route of the new metro service means it has to be relocated on to the site of a former school. It is being totally redeveloped at a cost of over £1 million.

A feasibility study for the redevelopment was funded by the Wythenshawe partnership and the Northwest Development Agency. The cost was £20,000 and it took seven to eight months to complete. The partnership was multi-agency and brought together public, private, voluntary and community sector organisations. Manchester City Council was the lead body in the partnership.

North Hulme Adventure Playground: Part of the basketball area with the under-sevens area and building in background
Photo by Manchester Adventure Play

The study itself was managed by Manchester Adventure Play (a charitable company funded predominately by Manchester City Council), and assisted by a small steering group comprising representatives of Benchill Adventure Playground, Wythenshawe Partnership, Northwest Development Agency, Manchester Youth Service, Early Years and Play Division and the City Planning Division.

The playground was completely rebuilt in 2000/1 with funding from Moss Side and Hulme SRB Partnership and other sources.

Early Years Development and Childcare Partnerships (EYDCPs)

Programmes for the expansion of childcare by EYDCPs can affect the way in which resources are allocated for children's play provision. They may also impact on the opportunities children and young people have for outdoor play. Increasing numbers of children up to 16 years old (14 if they have no particular special educational needs) are spending their free time in the care of people other than their parents. These carers need access to outdoor play facilities for young children and need to feel confident that older children in their care are safe.

Bath and North East Somerset: EYDCP supports outdoor play

Bath and North East Somerset Early Years Development and Childcare Partnership sees the provision of playgrounds and playground equipment as an important element of support for informal child carers in rural areas. To support this, the play development officer based in the EYDCP works with local authority leisure and parks departments, and the early years coordinator attends local authority planning meetings to promote the play and childcare needs of children in areas being redeveloped.

Community Safety Partnerships

Places where children feel safe to play can feel safer for everyone. Local safety schemes, including neighbourhood warden and park ranger schemes, have an important role to play in protecting children's opportunities for outdoor play.

Neighbourhood Renewal Partnerships

All neighbourhood renewal programmes will affect children's and young people's use of the outdoors. The partnerships have a key role in ensuring that the rights of children and young people to outdoor space are seen as equal to those of any other population group.

'In Vauxhall Park a couple of years ago you wouldn't have seen more than a few kids in the playground, and not a mum with small children to be seen – broken equipment and dog-fouled places kept most people away. Now thanks to a new dog-proof fence and restored and repaired equipment, new sports facilities and a wonderful new space-net climbing frame, there's lots for children of all ages in the park. There are now always children from all sections of the community to be seen enjoying themselves.'
Polly Freeman, mother of two under-fives

Lambeth: Play is part of neighbourhood renewal

In the London Borough of Lambeth children's play is seen as an integral part of the neighbourhood renewal process. Investing in better opportunities for children's play, particularly through the support and development of adventure playgrounds, is seen to:
- reduce unemployment through the employment of local staff;
- reduce crime;
- promote children's education and skills;
- promote better health;
- improve housing and the physical environment.

Early indications are that the Local Strategic Partnership will commission action research including extended weekend opening of selected adventure playgrounds and mapping play provision with a view to future improvement. Lambeth's Neighbourhood Renewal Programme is also supporting two other initiatives, a corporate play policy and strategy (see page 27) and a play and sports facility improvements programme (see page 24).

Children's Fund and Sure Start Partnerships.

The Children's Fund is delivering resources for the development of services to children and young people in areas of poverty and disadvantage. Local Children and Young People's Strategic Partnerships are developing 'non-stigmatising' services for children and young people aged 5–13 who are at risk of social exclusion through poverty and disadvantage. Sure Start partnerships are similar but focus on families with children under school age. A number of applications to the Children's Fund have included the potential expansion of children's play opportunities. These include Sheffield, Bradford, Tower Hamlets (London) and Leeds.

Leeds's Children's Fund proposal prioritises play

The application to the Fund from Leeds City Council, drawn from consultations with parents, children and young people, sees the need to address children's play opportunities as a central theme across the city. In almost every consultation with children and young people, their families and other local residents, the provision of safe play facilities and the improvement of existing ones was seen as a priority.

In order that play developments across Leeds are well coordinated the Children's Fund Team intends to fund a Play Development Project to:
- provide a source of advice, support and expertise on play projects, including funding sources and assistance in accessing them;

- employ development workers to work with local agencies to include play in local projects;
- provide a central point for the dissemination of information about training opportunities;
- support a forum for sharing good practice and to influence strategic planning within the local authority;
- enhance and build on more locally based projects targeted at communities with a high proportion of children at risk of becoming disadvantaged.

The cost of this proposal is estimated to be between £500,000 and £750,000 over two years.

In some areas voluntary sector and other local organisations are important providers

Voluntary sector and other local organisations, for example, play associations, parish councils and housing associations, are important providers of children's outdoor play space. Voluntary organisations, including local Groundwork Trusts and other environmental regeneration groups also have considerable expertise in the development of outdoor space. Many rural community councils have expertise in community development and are playing leading roles in initiatives such as Vital Villages and Market Town Initiatives.

Colshaw Scooter Time Trials, 2001

Macclesfield and Vale Royal: Groundwork projects give children and young people a sense of community involvement

The Colshaw Estate is a 1960s overspill estate for Manchester of 700 homes. It was left to its own devices for years, creating a run-down estate with few amenities for young people. Five years ago a plan was implemented by staff from Groundwork Macclesfield and Vale Royal with local people and agencies to improve facilities for the young people on the estate.

Surveys were carried out and workshops held on the estate to find out what the residents and young people felt was needed to address the problems. The young people stated that there was nothing to do and the adults felt that the young people were causing trouble, hanging around the streets of the estate. The young people on the streets were then consulted as to their issues and what facilities they would want in the community. The overwhelming results were for a skating area, sports pitch and somewhere to hang out.

A survey with the New Economics Foundation collected information to evaluate the possibility of implementing some of these ideas. The overwhelming response from the residents was to 'do anything to get the kids off our doorsteps'.

Designers try out new skate park facilities

Young people were asked 'What could it become?'
All photos by Peter Heberlet

Groundwork developed designs for the play area and held consultations with the children and young people. It was stressed to them that it would take a couple of years to obtain funding and construct. To keep their interest various initiatives were held such as an arts based project involving the children designing a large skateboard bench for their use. A week-long residential programme was also held to discuss the project in detail and develop team work with the group of young people.

Environmental issues were also introduced and a large planted area was created with young people of all ages helping. Ostensibly this was to shield the noise of the park from residents, but it was also to involve the younger children who one day would be the main users. By adding to the woodland near the site, the natural habitat of the area was increased.

A roller blade/bike track, half-pipe, basketball post and football pitch were installed. To begin with it was very heavily used and the residents complained as they had not realised so many children would be attracted to it. However, numbers soon decreased to a manageable level once the initial enthusiasm had worn off and the site continues to be used. Both residents and young people are now very happy with it and feel it has helped develop a community feel in the area. New initiatives are being developed with the community based around the youth centre including teenage shelter provision, again involving arts work and involvement of the young people at all stages.

Multi-disciplinary working supports effective planning and delivery

Multi-disciplinary planning groups offer opportunities for inter-agency coordinated planning for children's play and often lead to better communications generally between agencies and departments. This is particularly important in areas with two tiers of local government. A multi-agency, 'joined-up' approach is vital in taking forward corporate policy development and strategic planning.

Kingston-upon-Hull: agencies work together

The Patrington Haven Playground was built to cater for the needs of the local village that had no play provision. A large private sports and social complex had been built outside the village but was only open to the residents at a rate of £1000 a year. This had led to a lot of resentment in the community. The playground was developed by East Riding Local Authority and the residents of the village were involved in all stages of the consultation. The multi-agency approach involved representatives from East Riding Local Authority, the Regional Development Agency, Health Authority, Education Authority, Residents Association and Careers Forum.

This approach meant that the village got a facility of which they were proud and, more importantly, that they wished to use. The playground was developed along with a community centre and included the toddlers and under-eights area, as well as a hard court area with basketball posts and some cantilever swings for the older children. It is well used and still in very good condition. Sports development and play workers now run play schemes at the site during the holidays and after school.

Lambeth: departments come together to improve play and sport facilities

A joint initiative in 2001 between Lambeth's Education, Housing and Parks sections received £200,000 funding from the Neighbourhood Renewal Programme to improve unstaffed play and sports facilities in partnership with residents' associations and community groups. It is hoped to extend the programme, which has the slogan 'Making Lambeth a borough where children can be proud to grow up in', in conjunction with the new Lambeth Play Association to maximise inward investment by generating match-funding opportunities with grant making trusts and New Opportunities Fund lottery funding. Lambeth Play Development Service is also offering assistance for local groups to consult with children and young people.

Parents and other local residents need to be involved

Parents and other local adult residents need to be included in projects in addition to local agencies and children and young people. Some adults, especially local parents, may wish to see improvements in outdoor play opportunities, and have useful views and ideas. Other adults, particularly some local, older people, may have concerns about the presence of children and young people in public spaces, and may be anxious about the prospect of change.

In research asking children and young people and their parents about what things would make the neighbourhood better, children (particularly in inner and outer London) were very keen to see more play spaces and better kept surroundings, while parents wanted better security and traffic safety (O'Brien and others, 2000).

Little Dorrit Park in Bankside, before

Little Dorrit Playground, Bankside, Southwark: local parents lead the way

Little Dorrit Park in Bankside, London was first opened in 1902. It was created as an area specifically for children to play in a part of town notorious for its brothels, warehouses and destitution. The history of the park spurred a local group of parents and other volunteers into redeveloping a piece of ground that had become overlooked by the council and fallen into disrepair. The ground is surrounded by offices but has two nearby primary schools and a lot of local authority housing close by.

Southwark Council provided the majority of the funding through Capital Funding, whilst additional funds were raised through projects such as the Millennium Arts Project (£5000), local fundraising and small grants. In total they obtained upwards of £50,000.

The group began by consulting with local children in the area through after-school parties and big events within the park. At these events, which over 500 local children attended, entertainers and arts and crafts people were present, but the main consultation was in the form of a series of boards to which pictures of various play equipment (previously shortlisted by the group) were attached. The children were given stickers to stick on to their favourite pieces of equipment, which were described by activity rather than by technical terms. The group also used the Bankside Open Spaces Trust young peoples consultation project for 10- to 12-year-olds.

In order to cut down costs, the group did not employ an outside consultant but obtained advice from the council's landscape designer. The equipment that had been selected by the group for the exercise was chosen for its low cost, durability and safety.

The final pieces of equipment installed were: a small roundabout with a safety brake; climbing frame; metal train; and an under-fives area separated from the older children's space. A drinking fountain that had been amongst the children's highest priorities, but deemed unsuitable by the council, was also installed. A herb garden was also constructed out of three raised railway sleepers planted with child friendly herbs and plants, and today there is a gardening club at the site.

The play space has had almost no vandalism since it opened in 2000. The group feels that this is because the local families were involved throughout its design and the community are proud of what they see as their facility.

Little Dorrit Park in Bankside, after

All those involved need to agree shared values and principles

A key challenge facing those working to improve outdoor play opportunities is that stakeholder groups may start from very different points. For example, some children and young people may want to have the chance to spend time together away from adults, while some agencies may feel that they need more supervision over their activities. These potential differences need to be addressed as early as possible if projects or initiatives are to avoid becoming derailed at some later point.

In local authorities, the development and implementation of a corporate play policy, providing a framework for all types of indoor and outdoor play, provides a mechanism for clarifying values and principles. If it is to succeed, the policy must be 'owned' and signed up to by all those whose actions have an impact on children's free time. Moreover, strategies around outdoor play cannot work in isolation and must be linked closely with other relevant local strategies and developments.

Developing and agreeing key criteria for the development of children's play may require time and negotiation. The central focus must always remain the play needs of children and young people. Children's play policies should have clear links to other strategies and should be integral elements of local cultural strategies.

Advantages for a 'provider' in having a functioning play policy

- agreed principles and definitions;
- focus on children;
- transparency;
- local commitment;
- a necessary first step;
- a basis for quality;
- a foundation for safety;
- a framework for the allocation of resources;
- consistency between training and practice.

Source: adapted from Melville, 1998

Bath and North East Somerset develop a play policy
Development of Bath and North East Somerset's play policy began in 1999, initiated by the Youth and Community Services Department. A working party included elected members, officers from education, strategic planning, housing, social services, youth and community, parks, sports and early years sections, and representatives from local voluntary sector play and children's organisations. The resulting policy document covers a range of children's play opportunities, including staffed adventure playgrounds, non-staffed fixed equipment playgrounds, activity centres, play centres, holiday play schemes and clubs, out-of-school childcare provision schools and early childhood provision.

Lambeth: neighbourhood renewal supports corporate play policy and strategy work
With support from Neighbourhood Renewal funds, Lambeth is developing a corporate play policy and strategy to inform strategic thinking about children's play needs. The emphasis is on children who are likely to have restricted access or inadequate opportunities for play. To achieve this the council, in conjunction with all relevant partners, will seek to maximise external investment and ensure through consultation that local play needs are met.

2.2 Involving children and young people

Key points in this section:

- It is as important for children and young people to be involved in local planning decisions as it is for adults
- The participation of children and young people can have wide ranging benefits
- Different levels of involvement and participation are appropriate in different circumstances
- Adults involved need to be skilled and have the right attitudes
- There are basic principles common to all types of participation
- Methods will depend on the aims and objectives of the process
- Children and young people can be involved from the very early stages
- When redesigning or altering a play space, children and young people can be involved from the very early stages
- Some groups of children and young people may need targeted attention

It is as important for children and young people to be involved in local planning decisions as it is for adults

Most new Government funding streams and initiatives require that local people are consulted and involved. Children and young people can be asked for their ideas and views via questionnaires, focus groups, meetings, conferences, children's councils, special events, poster competitions and drama presentations. In some areas children and young people are actively involved in the planning, development and running of services for themselves and others.

Amongst the young people Matthews and others interviewed in Northamptonshire in the mid 1990s, only 26 per cent had ever talked to anyone about ways in which they would like to see their local area altered and this was mainly to parents, friends and relatives. When asked why this was, over half said they had never thought about it, one in 10 said they did not know who to contact and one in 10 did not think anyone would listen (Matthews and others, 1998).

If the participation of children and young people is sought and respected as part of the planning, development and maintenance of outdoor environments the result is likely to be:
- better environments for everyone;
- better targeted play services and provision;
- better informed adults;
- more satisfied children and young people;
- opportunities for all children and young people whatever their interests and abilities;
- children and young people with increased skills and knowledge;

■ a sense of ownership amongst children and young people, fostering greater respect for the environment;

■ less vandalism and fewer complaints from other community members.

The experience children and young people have of their neighbourhoods and surroundings is often very different from the adult perception. Children and young people who are out and about a lot often know more about their neighbourhood than older people. They know about the special 'hidden' places and come across threats to the environment missed by adults. Finding out from children and young people about ways in which a neighbourhood can be improved is a sound basis for making it a better place for everyone.

Views on the value of children's participation	
An adult perspective	**Some children's perspectives**
Professionals should be interested in and sensitive to children's perspectives because: ■ children are members of society and have a right to be involved in matters that affect them; ■ children use many public services and can offer informed opinions about their experiences of them; ■ sometimes children can offer a new perspective; helping to improve services; ■ involvement improves relationships between adults and children; ■ children learn to respect others through being respected for their opinions and contributions.	A group of children summarised the benefits of consultation within democracy: ■ when young people and adults mix, it leads to a better atmosphere and less chance of disruption; ■ young people have a part to play as members of their community; ■ young people have needs but also responsibilities: too often this aspect is forgotten; ■ young people need the support of sympathetic adults; ■ young people need advice and information in a way that they can understand; ■ an investment in young people as future citizens would benefit the whole community.

Source: Freeman and others, 1999

Different levels of involvement and participation are appropriate in different circumstances

There is no one best model or method for involving children and young people. The most appropriate method depends on the types of discussion and decisions being undertaken. Sometimes it might be appropriate merely to solicit views and ideas to inform general planning. At other times children and young people might have control of the whole financial and decision-making process.

Examples of where different levels of participation might be appropriate

Possible circumstances	Aim of participation
Intention to build a by-pass across the fields near a village	Getting a child or young person's perspective on a general planning issue
Proposals to change the traffic flow in a residential area	Finding out views on decisions which will directly affect them
Development of a play policy and implementation strategy	Establishing what children and young people would like from the services or provision specifically for them
Redevelopment of a local playground	Involving children and young people in the planning and development of services for them
Development and running of a 'special interest' project such as an arts project	Involving children and young people in project planning, management, and service delivery
Development and running of youth centres and youth cafés, environmental projects	Children and adults working as partners in service planning and delivery
Youth cafés, special interest activities, clubs	Children and young people having control of budgets, decisions and all other aspects of the project

Some of the Shoreditch children's messages:

'I live in a place which is loud and dirty and attractive to slugs, snails, insects, rats and all kinds of beasts! There are drug sellers in one of the blocks. The place I live in is simply dangerous. I'd like it all to change. I want the place I live in to be clean, quiet with no nasty creatures and no drug sellers.'

'...to improve parks in Shoreditch because they are totally boring.'

'I would like a little park in my flats because all there is only a little square in front of my flats and there is lots of kids in my flats and sometimes we are very bored when we don't have anything to do. I would like a slide, swings, roundabout and a climbing frame.'

Shoreditch: participation leads to real change

In Shoreditch, an inner London urban area, children have very limited access to play spaces and many of those that do exist are subject to potential closure. Save the Children (SCF) and Shoreditch Our Way (SHOW) – formerly Shoreditch New Deal Trust – are attempting to rectify this. With 5000 young people in the immediate area they carried out a consultation survey with over 300 children between the ages of three and ten to see what they would want to change and improve in Shoreditch.

The very young children took photographs of what they did and did not like, or recorded their comments and made artwork about their environment. The older children wrote messages to SHOW about what they wanted the New Deal for Communities money to be spent on.

Over 1000 messages were written, 150 children completed drawings or posters and over 40 children from nurseries were involved in taking photographs. The largest number of messages were about play and enjoying oneself (353), followed by safety (222), education (192), health (140) and the environment (127).

On completion of the consultation work SCF, in partnership with local young children, produced a list of 11 recommendations for projects that children want to see happen in Shoreditch. In February 2002 the full board of SHOW agreed to adopt all 11 recommendations within their 2002–5 delivery plan. This demonstrates SHOW's commitment to listen to the youngest members of the community.

Adults involved need to be skilled and have the right attitudes

Not everyone has the skills, attitudes and experience necessary to support the successful and effective participation. All those involved in the process need to understand the importance of what they are doing and have the necessary skills and expertise. They also need real support and commitment from senior managers if their time and efforts are to have any real impact.

There are basic principles common to all types of participation

'No one's 'hard to reach'. You just have to go out and talk to them.'
Outreach youth worker

There are some common principles for success, whatever the method of participation used. If these are not accepted and adopted, the process may, at best, be superficial and at worst result in bored, disillusioned children and young people whose confidence in the democratic process is seriously undermined.

Successful involvement of children and young people requires:
- commitment from adults and a willingness to learn from children and young people;

- agreed objectives that address the questions why, what, who, when, where, how;
- recognition that the process is as important as the outcome;
- Willingness to involve children and young people in the development of process and methodology;
- open discussion and mutual agreement about ethical issues and the 'rules' of the process;
- open discussion about will happen as a result of the process and what feedback and evaluation is planned;
- an understanding of the limitations and parameters surrounding the participation and follow-up to avoid realising unrealistic expectations;
- ensuring the children and young people are given all relevant information so they can give informed views;
- a methodology appropriate to the aims of the process and the aims and previous experience of the children and young people; for some children this might involve working with people with specialist knowledge or skills;
- an understanding that children and young people grow up, move on and their interests change so, for many, long-term change may be of little relevance or interest;
- recognition that children and young people need quick results so they can see and experience the effects of their involvement.

For a six-year-old child, a three-year delay is half a lifetime and a five-year delay is almost a whole lifetime. The needs of a six-year-old and an 11-year-old are significantly different as are the needs of a nine- or 14-year-old. Therefore, the timescale from the design to implementation needs to be short if particular children are to be involved in ensuring that specific facilities are going to meet their needs. On broader, estate-wide issues, an alternative strategy might be to involve as many groups as possible to ensure the broadest range of views (Wheway and Millward, 1997).

Methods will depend on the aims and objectives of the process

Children and young people are capable of identifying their own needs, planning for change, raising funds and providing practical efforts to improve their estates and neighbourhoods. The real challenge is for those in charge of these processes to welcome them and support them in that process. One approach is to identify someone on the design team to act as a mentor and liaison point for the children and young people.

Initially it is worth talking informally as well as formally with the children and young people, employed staff and parents. Observing ways the existing space, facilities and equipment are used adds to the knowledge base. It gives insights into activities and behaviours that children and young people do not wish to reveal or forget about when formally asked.

'Children are very good at pleasing adults. When we ask them questions they will try to give us answers that show they know and understand the way adults see the world. From a very early age children have been taken to places the adults call playgrounds and told that what they can do there is "play". It is not surprising therefore that when we ask them what kind of play possibilities they want at their playground they ask for more of what they already know to be in playgrounds.'
Hendricks, 2001

Camden Street Park welcome panel – a fusion of local children community arts workers and steel fabricators

Local children enjoying the new facility in Graham Street
Photo by the Dojo 2000 Community Group

Talking with children and young people who do not use the space about whether or not they might want to if suitable changes are made will add to the general picture of how the space might best be developed. As ideas develop they can be tried out with the children to find out their views on how the changes would work.

Walsall: children and young people help to improve playgrounds

In Walsall, over the past 10 years a number of playgrounds in public areas have been improved through the involvement of local children. In Camden Street Park the Leisure and Community Services Department worked with children from the local schools to create an arts-based playsite. The children were involved in writing the signage for the park as well as choosing the theme for the design. They chose a nature theme that included insects like ladybirds incorporated in the rubber floor of the playground. At Bentley West Playing Fields young people were involved from the very beginning. A competition was held in the school overlooking the playing field to choose a design for the play area. There was one outstanding winner – a jigsaw design – which was well received by the contractors due to its simplicity and flexibility. Drawing in the local school children enabled the play areas to become a part of the community, and as a result vandalism has been limited.

Birmingham: Groundwork involves children and young people in a range of play projects

Groundwork UK Barclays SiteSaver projects have undertaken a range of local development projects with children and young people. These have included three projects developed in Birmingham during 2000 and 2001.

Grosvenor and Westminster Community garden was a derelict inner city site. Groundwork Birmingham supported the Grosvenor and Westminster Garden Group – made up of local residents, young and old – in developing a play area and attractive garden. This included a slide, play surfacing, planting and a willow shelter. The local community were involved in all aspects of the project. It is a secure site and local residents are key holders.

At Graham Street a basketball and multi-use court was developed next door to a community centre. Again the local children and community were involved in consultation, and it was agreed they wanted a multi-use sports court. Today up to 50 children every night regularly use the facility and local crime has been reduced.

2.2 Involving children and young people

The remains of the original ball court
Photo by the Dojo 2000 Community Group

The former Hockley Adventure Playground, a prominent piece of public land that had been abandoned, has also been improved. The size of the site is perfect for a popular recreational facility, which are in short supply in the area. In order to start the improvement, community 'clear-up' events were held by Groundwork Birmingham in conjunction with the local community group Dojo 2000. The first priority for the site was for the erection of strong perimeter fencing and gates to stop vandalism and fly tipping. Basketball hoops and goals were also installed. In the next phase, play equipment is to be returned to the site and an on-site community officer will be on hand to lead the project. Work continues to convert the land into a recreational park.

above: Hockley Adventure Playground after one of the community clear-up events
below: The new multi-use goals
Photos by the Dojo 2000 Community Group

Methods for developing the participation of children and young people

Method	Purpose
Children's conferences	Opportunity for delegates to share ideas and projects and develop future directions and initiatives. Multi-media and video conferencing present further opportunities.
Surveys and consultation exercises	Obtain information and feedback necessary in developing child-aware services and structures.
Access days; children's days	For a specified time each year, usually a day or a week, children's programmes are organised in which children's activities are prioritised and children are able to voice their concerns to leaders and officials at all levels of government.
Youth councils/fora	Meetings of young people who come together, usually as a committee, to voice their views about their social and physical environments.
Newsletters, circulars and information leaflets	Promote information exchange, represent children's views and focus on subjects of interest to children.
Information exchange facilities	Places for young people to meet, obtain information and investigate opportunities for participation.

The direct involvement of one of the local children in the improvements, Birmingham

Partnerships	To combine the expertise, resources and experience of several partners to their mutual benefit.
Research	Acquires the data necessary for developing child-focused plans, strategies, policies and practice.
Action plans and strategies	Develop future plans and initiatives that reflect children's perspectives and needs.
Websites, videos, photo exhibitions, audio-visual or other new media projects	Allow children to use sound, images and text to get their messages across in new, exciting, engaging ways.
Focus groups	Where children come together with or without professionals to address particular issues.

Source: adapted from Freeman and others, 1999

When redesigning or altering a play space, children and young people can be involved from the very early stages

The starting point must be finding out if local children and young people, both those who use the space and those who do not, think changes are necessary. If they do not, questions should be asked about whose needs are being addressed. If other vested interests are stronger and changes are to be made anyway, the concerns and impact on the children and young people must be addressed.

Dunkeswell: 'Playing for Real' – something for everyone

Devon@Play tries 'Playing for Real'

In Devon several play areas have been developed using the 'Playing for Real' process, inspired by the 'Planning for Real' planning technique. Both use scale models as a basis for discussion.

At the request of the local community a Devon@Play worker visits the play site with a group of local children. The children are asked what they like and dislike about the site, how they access it and what they wish to do when they play. The group then go to an indoor venue where there is a short discussion and an opportunity to look at varied display material. Questionnaires are given to the children, who are helped to complete them.

The practical session begins with setting out a 'map' of the play on either cloth, sand or clean compost. The children then create models using modelling and scrap materials of features and equipment they would like to see on the site. Finally, the model is discussed and a consensus reached on the most important aspects of the design.

The playworker uses this information to write a report on the children's views, which is given to the community, parish council or local authority. Usually only some of the ideas produced in a 'Playing for Real' are utilised. At Brentor, for example, the four-arm swing, the mound, the zip wire and the willow tunnel were effected. The willow tunnel design evolved from the input of children and other participants while it was being made.

'Playing for Real' draws adults and children together to discuss and plan; it also uncovers local solutions. It adds credibility to the planning group (useful if there is local opposition) and helps break down barriers because it is a fun activity. 'Playing for Real' improves the organisation's knowledge of local action and provides contacts that are particularly useful for remote rural locations. The team have not experienced any negative reactions to the process – most people say it is informative and are impressed by the contribution of the children. Devon@Play is now developing a 'Skating for Real' process to help communities plan skate parks.

Brentor – 'Playing for Real', models become reality

Some groups of children and young people will need targeted attention

Participation processes will need to give targeted thought and attention to children and young people with disabilities, and those from black and minority ethnic groups, if their concerns are to be properly addressed.

There are disabled children and young people in every community, although they may not be highly visible. They need to be able to use the same play spaces as their non-disabled peers. Frequently, disabled children and young people are isolated and marginalised, sometimes only ever having contact with other disabled children and young people in special schools and holiday provision. Identifying the access needs of these children and young people often requires the help and support of these specialist centres and of the children's parents, carers or independent advocates.

If outdoor play spaces are to be truly accessible and attractive to all, the consultation process must actively involve children and young people with different needs, including those who:
- use wheelchairs (both manual and electric, accompanied and independently);
- use crutches or sticks;
- have restricted, little or no sight;
- have impaired hearing or are deaf;
- use non-verbal means of communication;
- have limited movement of any sort;
- have learning or cognitive difficulties.

Many children and young people from black and minority communities may have concerns around culture or racism, but may not feel comfortable discussing these issues in culturally or ethnically mixed groups of people. Participation processes should be designed to allow people from a range of cultural or ethnic groups to spend some time in separate groups, if they wish, to explore these issues, rather than assume they will emerge naturally.

2.3 Developing objectives

Key points in this section:

- Projects need to have clear aims and objectives
- Objectives should be SMART

Projects need to have clear aims and objectives

Developing aims and objectives:
- helps clarify what it is hoped will be achieved;
- ensures the process of planning and decision making is transparent and easy for others to understand;
- makes it easier to evaluate the success of the initiative.

Objectives should be SMART

Whilst the aims of the development process give a vision and framework for guiding planning, the objectives describe the tasks involved in realising the vision. Objectives should be:

Specific: clearly defined and easy to understand.

Measurable: in order to achieve your objectives, you must identify how you will measure them.

Achievable: your objectives should be achievable within the timescale you anticipate.

Resourced: you will only achieve your objectives if you have the resources to deliver them or know where those resources will come from.

Timed: thinking through the timetable for delivery of each objective will help ensure its achievability.

In its guidance on developing Community Strategies the Government suggests a series of key aims. The aims for developing children's and young people's outdoor play space can be very similar.

Aims for developing children's and young people's outdoor play space.

A local outdoor play strategy should:
- allow local communities, especially children and young people (based upon geography and/or interest) to articulate their aspirations, needs and priorities;
- coordinate the actions of the council, and of the public, private, voluntary and community organisations that operate locally;
- focus and shape existing and future activity of those organisations so that they effectively meet children's and young people's needs and aspirations;
- contribute to the achievement of local sustainable development.

Key components:
- a long-term vision for the area focusing on the outcomes that are to be achieved;

'Wildlife' theme, as chosen by local children, incorporated into flooring and street furniture at Camden Street Park, Walsall

- an action plan identifying short-term priorities and activities that will contribute to the achievement of long-term outcomes;
- a shared commitment to implement the action plan and proposals for doing so;
- arrangements for monitoring the implementation of the action plan, for periodically reviewing the community strategy, and for reporting progress to local communities.

Source: adapted from DETR, 2000b

2.4 Addressing barriers

Key points in this section:

- Providers of dedicated play spaces should take a balanced approach to safety
- Insurance cover is a key issue
- Conflicts over space need to be addressed
- Land ownership and potential must be checked and clarified

Providers of dedicated play spaces should take a balanced approach to safety

Many children and young people want exciting, challenging play opportunities with a degree of risk. This can be at odds with the concerns of providers, who may be more worried about liability in the event of accidents. What is needed is a balanced approach to manage the risks so that children's wishes can be met while protecting them from serious harm. In this way the risk of losses from legal action can also be managed. Equipment standards and guidance are helpful in informing decisions, as part of a reasonable approach to safety and risk management (Davies and Heseltine, 2000). European standards and Health and Safety Executive guidance provide clear standards for the safety of playground equipment (Heseltine, 1998; Heseltine, 2000).

The Play Safety Forum, a body that brings together the leading national organisations involved in play safety, has drawn up and agreed a position statement on the need to take a balanced approach to safety in play provision, entitled *Managing Risks in Play Provision* (Play Safety Forum, 2002). In summary form the statement says: 'Children need and want to take risks when they play. Play provision aims to respond to these needs and wishes by offering children stimulating, challenging environments for exploring and developing their abilities. In doing this, play provision aims to manage the level of risk so that children are not exposed to unacceptable risks of death or serious injury.' The full statement is available from the Children's Play Council.

A suitable and sufficient risk assessment, skilled installation and on-going inspections and maintenance are vital elements in the manage-ment of any dedicated play space. Providers are likely to be liable on the grounds of negligence if a child has an accident or is injured on one of their sites that has not been properly inspected and maintained.

Every dedicated outdoor play space should therefore have a regular inspection and maintenance programme. In some areas this might involve daily cleaning and inspections backed up by routine weekly maintenance programmes. In others, the regime may be less intensive but must nevertheless be appropriate and rigorous. Public notices on sites, giving information about when routine inspection and maintenance procedures are to be or have been carried out, are useful both to children and young people and to their parents. Information, especially telephone numbers, about where problems can be reported by the public can also help providers maintain their sites to a high standard and demonstrate their commitment to doing so.

Insurance cover is a key issue

Sometimes potentially excellent play equipment or resources are not provided because of fears of litigation and/or fears that they cannot be insured. The advent of 'no win, no fee' legal claims is having an impact on play spaces as in other areas of public services. But insurers for local authorities report that the levels of litigation involving play space are low compared to other issues such as pavement slips, trips and falls. This suggests that the fears about litigation are more significant than the actual risk of legal action following accidental injury. The question of risk management is a large one for local authorities and other providers and the debates are continuing. However, providers of well-designed, well-built and well-maintained play spaces that are understood and valued by local children and parents, are less likely to be challenged.

Conflicts over space need to be addressed

Most public outdoor space is used by many different individuals and groups. The needs and behaviour of one group of people should not unnecessarily restrict the access and use of the space by another. Potential conflicts of interest between children and young people and adults must be addressed in the early planning stages. If they are not they will almost certainly cause problems later on.

'Please do something about our area because we are all classed as delinquents but we are not. We want somewhere to go. Thank you.'
A 14-year-old female

Children and young people often feel they are denied access to open spaces by adults who want to restrict their activities, while adults frequently cite the behaviour of children and young people as one of the most common problems they face when outdoors. Participation and involvement processes need to be able to cope with this.

It is unlikely that one solution will emerge that everyone supports, so the process needs to enable groups to reach acceptable compromises. It may also be unrealistic to expect that change will completely remove conflict or problems over public space. Children and young people – and adults – do not always behave reasonably. However, good participation processes should bring different groups together and help them understand each other's points of view, thus enabling communities to resolve more minor conflicts and disagreements themselves.

In some ways, the play and outdoor play activities of children and young people today are not very different from those of their parents and grandparents when they were young – each generation has activities that are 'disapproved of' by the previous ones. But today, because of busy lifestyles, longer working hours, more individual transport in cars, warm homes and other indoor attractions, adults no longer get to know local children as they grow up; young people and adults may have no idea how to relate to each other in an informal, friendly manner. Young people are aware that their presence, when out and about in groups in the neighbourhood, sometimes feels threatening to others.

Young people sometimes use younger children's play areas for their own games or as places to sit and talk. They also sometimes leave their litter and debris behind, offending adults who feel a bad example and dangerous place is being left for their young children. This can cause conflict between adults, who feel their younger children are being excluded from use of the playground, and young people.

For some young people playgrounds may well be the only 'children's' space they have access to and are familiar with, and the only place to sit when there is nowhere else they feel welcome or where they can meet friends undisturbed. Most young people do not wish to cause a nuisance but merely to find somewhere they can spend time. Young people need places where they can be sometimes visible, sometimes not; where they can meet their friends and enjoy themselves.

'I speak to my friends a lot about our childhood. Half the time is taken up talking about how the youth of today are such a horrible lot, the other half by stories about the horrible things we got up to. Still the penny doesn't drop.'
Tovell, 2000

Young people say that:
- children and young people and adults are often concerned about the same issues but may have differing perspectives and strengths of feeling;
- young people and adults should work together not against each other;
- young people and adults have a tendency to stereotype and scapegoat each other rather than address common problems;
- young people and adults need to work harder to understand each other's points of view.

Source: Freeman and others 1999

Land ownership and potential must be checked and clarified

Issues of land ownership and future use can often be complex and must be clarified before any formal development of children's and young people's outdoor play space. It is not unknown for new projects to be developed with children and young people, for example, on apparently disused land, and to be abruptly halted when the land is taken away for some other, newly-agreed purpose. Before embarking on any new developments for outdoor space the ownership of the land, both freehold and leasehold, should be identified and all proposed future uses clarified and agreed (NPFA, 2001). Current planning consents should also be established.

2.5 Establishing what needs to be done

Key points in this section:

- An outdoor play audit is essential
- The audit needs to find out who the local children and young people are, where they play and why they play there
- The audit needs to investigate all relevant outdoor space

An outdoor play audit is essential

Opportunities for children's outdoor play are affected by the actions of many local authority departments, partnerships and developments. Any one of these may only have a partial picture of existing provision. Moreover, any changes need to be based on robust information about where children and young people are playing and why. An outdoor play audit will help to ensure that agencies have the information they need, and that children and young people have sufficient and appropriate places for their outdoor activities. Outdoor play audits involve a detailed examination of what exists now and what children and young people feel would increase their outdoor play opportunities.

The audit needs to find out who the local children and young people are, where they play and why they play there

Who are the local children and young people?
The first step in assessing local needs is to find out about the local population of children and young people. For example:

- What is their age?
- Where do they live?
- What are their cultural and ethnic backgrounds?

The only reliable way to establish what local children and young people want and need from outdoor play space is through a combination of asking them, asking their parents and other community members and observing their activities.

Both quantitative and qualitative research and analysis may be required to identify the needs and aspirations of children and young people. Quantitative research is required to establish the numbers of children and young people, and the cultural norms and differences within the child and the family population. Qualitative research provides information about the actual behaviour of individual children and is more appropriate for in-depth investigations of attitudes, opinions and experiences. Quantitative and qualitative work combined can provide descriptions of behaviour by interest group, age group, locality, gender and race (Moore, 1990).

Where are the children and young people playing now?
As they grow up children and young people tend to play increasingly further away from their homes. Whilst younger children in particular may spend most of their play time where they can see and be seen, playing in places which are in open view of houses, older children and young people

tend to seek out places where they are away from the gaze and scrutiny of adults.

In addition, as children grow older and play away from home, the distances from home vary. Whilst some children continue to play indoors because of the physical circumstances or because they prefer indoor activities, other children spend little of their free time at home, choosing instead to play outdoors, exploring and moving about. Children who ride bikes and or live in suburban areas tend to go further from home than others. Outdoors, children and young people may spend relatively short amounts of time in specifically designed play spaces. Much of their time is spent moving from place to place and much play takes place 'en route' rather than in designated play areas (Wheway and Millward, 1997).

Children and young people from minority ethnic and cultural groups may have distinct concerns about play spaces. For example, they may be subject to racial harassment in some spaces, or may avoid them because they feel that their presence will not be welcomed.

Haringey children plan their play space

Children from the Northumberland Park estate say what they want using a model of their neighbourhood

Haringey children give the zipwire a thumbs-up

Northumberland Park Estate, Haringey: children are the experts

In 2001, 28 children from school years six and nine from the London Borough of Haringey worked with Haringey Play Association to plan the refurbishment of their local outdoor play space. The children's schools saw the project as important enough to allow them to take part during school hours. The principles underpinning the consultation methods used were discovery, empowerment, democracy and inclusion.

The children, who were seen as the primary experts in play, took part in 'fact-finding' trips, workshops, and model-making. The children visited the designated space in the centre of their housing estate where they examined, measured and criticised it. They then constructed a model of the existing space on which they tested different ideas and proposals. The children's plans included facilities for babies and elderly people and environmental improvements, including a community garden, ponds and a quiet area as well as play and youth facilities. They also modelled their ideas for play structures. To ensure the children's expectations were not inhibited by limited experience, they visited and evaluated six different playgrounds.

Once all the information had been gathered the children made proposals for developing the site, voted on each other's ideas and developed ideas for the development that were both realistic and achievable. These are now under consideration.

Gloucestershire undertakes a play space audit

A specially-convened Neighbourhood Children's Commission, supported by Gloucestershire Neighbourhood Project Network, the EYDCP and White City Adventure Playground Association, aimed to use the voice of children in its audit of play space in Gloucestershire. A playworker was appointed to visit eight housing areas in Gloucestershire where, with the aid of community workers, he met and talked to local children about where they played and what play space was available. Children acted as the guides in each area. A written report and slide show were presented to the Commission.

A filmmaker recorded the playworker's travels and independently interviewed children and playworkers in each area. An independent research body established 24 focus groups; each of the eight areas held three, a young child, a teenager and an adult group. Statistical research on childcare, playgroup and after-school provision is also being compiled and will be added to the Commission's report.

The collected evidence (in the form of reports and films) was heard at a Commission Day. Over 60 people attended the Day and took part in the debate that followed. The meeting was presided over by eight Commissioners, a body that included young people, and a final report from them is pending. The Day itself was also filmed and will act as further evidence towards the report's conclusions.

Despite highlighting a lack of provision and understanding of play space and children's needs, there was also evidence of good practice. Many of those involved in the research and Commission Day have felt a sea change in their attitude to children's play. Action is already underway in some areas as a direct consequence of hearing children's voices.

Somerset bike tracks get well used

Unsupervised dedicated play spaces

Most children and young people play in playgrounds at some time although the location and design can often mean they are not well used by disabled children. Playgrounds are often located in parks and other green spaces or in residential areas near children's homes.

Children are more likely to use playgrounds in parks and other green spaces when they are with adults but tend to use those nearer their homes when they are out on their own or with their friends. This may be the result of lack of safe pedestrian routes or suitable public transport linking their homes to play provision in parks.

Factors influencing playground use include the age and interest of the local children and young people; location; the range, type and condition of the equipment and surfaces; how well they are cleaned and maintained and what other play opportunities there are locally.

Areas for cycling, skateboarding, skating and scootering are also popular, particularly with boys. Where there are no attractive facilities for 'play on wheels', children and young people will use the streets, curbs, walls, and steps they can find, frequently to the disapproval of adults.

'They treat you like you are grown up here at the adventure playground. They listen to you and do the sorts of things that you want.'

Staffed outdoor play settings

A small proportion of children regularly use open access, staffed play provision such as adventure playgrounds, play centres and holiday play schemes. Where it exists, open access staffed play provision tends to be well used and popular with both children and parents. Parents are confident that children are both enjoying themselves and safe and children have a wide range of play opportunities. Other open access facilities offering children play opportunities include city farms and wildlife and nature reserves.

Commercial play settings

As opportunities for children to play outside freely and on their own diminish, so the development of privately owned and commercial play spaces increases. Many private businesses with public access, for example pubs, shopping centres and private parks now offer dedicated play spaces for children. There is also an increase in pay-for-use playgrounds and sports facilities. The cost of these is, however, a deterrent for children from families with low incomes and increases the disadvantage they experience. The move away from free, drop-in neighbourhood provision to large-scale, commercial play centres increases the social exclusion of significant numbers of children and young people and where it exists, it should be monitored in the audit.

Gardens

Where they have them children do use their gardens to play in. However, if they are keen to play with or meet their friends, the garden is not always the best location for this. Children sometimes prefer playing in their front garden, rather than at the back, so they can see their friends passing and make contact with them.

Streets

Children have always played in the streets and roads outside or near their homes. Recent research shows that, despite safety fears and public education campaigns, the most common place for children's outdoor play is the streets near their homes. For example, research on housing estates in the mid-1990s found that children tended to spend much of their free time out-of-doors in the streets, partly because they could more easily meet their friends there and partly because much of the time they are moving about in search of others (Wheway and Millward, 1997). Another study in Northamptonshire found that young people frequently used the streets as a 'place to be' because there was nothing else for them to do in the locality (Matthews and others, 1998). Two surveys carried out in 2001 found that children played out on the streets more often than anywhere else, even if this was not always their preferred play space (Child Accident Prevention Trust, 2001; Children's Play Council and The Children's Society, 2001).

Other outdoor spaces
Although many children play in the outdoor places near their homes a significant proportion do not make use of the wealth of play opportunities these can offer. This might be because the places are inaccessible, thought to be unsafe or because the children and young people are prohibited from using them by adults. Where they exist, children may well be playing in many places not specifically designed for them, for example, cemeteries, allotments, building sites, canals and reservoirs. Other neighbourhood places where children might be playing include natural features such as rivers, banks, fields, hedges and woodlands, school grounds that are open to the public, roadside edges and the edges of common ground, sports fields, small parks and areas that are being made ready for reclamation and redevelopment. Areas of wasteland, greenways and natural environments can be important outdoor play spaces as can footpaths, pavements and pedestrian and cycle routes, which can provide smooth surfaces for wheeled activities such as skates, skateboards and scooters.

Children's use of the local neighbourhood as a play space depends on who and where they are. One survey found that children in inner and outer London were most likely to play out in local green spaces but also used the street or pavement, their own or other people's gardens and the local neighbourhood. But those in Hatfield (a commuter belt new town north of London) were more likely to play out on the street or pavement than in local green spaces. The children from Hatfield also used their own and other people's private gardens more (O'Brien and others, 2000).

Some children and young people cycle to play and to get to their play spaces. Much cycling takes place near homes and children and young people with roadworthy bikes also use them as part of their everyday routines for moving quickly around between different places where they play.

Children and young people moving about between their play places do not always use the 'official' roads and paths but frequently find their own routes. These might be seen as quick or interesting ways of getting somewhere and might involve climbing through holes and fences or over walls and gates. They are an important part of the excitement and exploration of outdoor play.

Parks and other green spaces

Parks, village greens and recreation grounds are some of the most popular places for children and young people. For young people these are places they can go to for free and are sometimes used for this reason. Parks and other green spaces are also seen by young people as refuges away from problems caused by the adults who resent their presence in other public areas such as shopping precincts and town centres.

In some areas the most frequent users of parks and other green spaces are young people who use them as places to meet their friends and talk. Young people know about these spaces because they used them as children and some young people spend most of their free time in them, especially in summer. Where parks and other green spaces are well designed and maintained, children and young people see them as relatively safe environments, compared with the streets where they often feel they are not welcome.

In rural areas village greens and recreation grounds are popular. These may or may not have equipment and sometimes fulfil a similar role to urban parks in the lives of rural children and young people.

Haringey children give the rope swing a star

Northumberland Park, Haringey: plans take shape

Environmental play at Brentor, Devon

O'Brien and others found that in inner London 89 per cent of the children and young people in their study were within walking distance of a park, compared with 95 per cent of those in outer London and 91 per cent of those in the new town. Thirty per cent of the children living in inner London had no private garden, whilst only 3 per cent of those in outer London and 1 per cent of those in new towns had no garden. Almost half the children in the study had visited a park in the previous week (O'Brien and others, 2000).

Why are the children and young people choosing those places to play?

Children and young people's play patterns are influenced by their relationships with their parents, family and friends, how much they like to watch television and use computer games, the cultural attitudes in the community towards play and children being outdoors, the perception of social and physical hazards in the surrounding environment, the influence of school, other opportunities for them locally and the attitudes and abilities and interest of each individual child. The only way to find out the complex needs is to observe and ask.

Children and young people who live a few streets or even a few doors from each other may have completely different patterns of play. Even children in the same household do not necessarily play in the same places or in the same ways.

In assessing need it is as important to work with children and watch their behaviour, as it is to ask them questions. Although they might describe the places where they play, children on the way to a certain place often get very involved in playing 'en route' so that the object of their journey in the first place can become lost (Moore, 1990). It is also important to identify children's needs at different times of the week and the year, and to consider how needs might change as the population of children and young people either grow up or move on. Casual observations and general discussions with groups of children who come forward to be involved may not ensure that the needs of all local and visiting children and young people are included in the assessment of need.

All play provision must be accessible and attractive to children and young people with a wide range of physical, learning and sensory abilities. It may be necessary to seek out and consult with those with specialist experience and knowledge, possibly outside the local community.

Children asked to consider an ideal place to play in an urban area of Birmingham mentioned parks and playgrounds (particularly adventure playgrounds), gardens with flowers, grassy fields and proper sports pitches. Other places included nature reserves, dumps where dens could be made and zoos. Equipment was not necessarily an important factor in children's popular places to play although swings, slides, climbing frames and roundabouts were popular. There were important social factors in children's identification of their ideal places. Boys and girls were equally concerned that there should be provision for smaller children as well as the older ones, others wanted to stop vandalism and they wanted to play in places which were free of dogs and broken glass (Wheway and Millward, 1997).

The audit needs to investigate all relevant outdoor space

The outdoor play space audit needs to establish:
- exactly what spaces currently exist;
- how children and young people use those spaces;
- what plans already exist for the development of local spaces generally.

What spaces currently exist

Whilst most of the existing play space will have been identified when finding out where children and young people play there may be some areas, recorded as play spaces by the local authority or parish council, which are closed or not well used. These should also be recorded in the audit.

How are children and young people using the spaces?

The following questions can help clarify children's and young people's use of space.
- Do all children and young people have ready access to play spaces appropriate to their age, interests, cultural needs and physical, learning and sensory abilities?
- How well is existing space currently used by different groups of children and young people? What are the reasons behind the ways in which children and young people currently use the spaces?
- Where is existing provision in relation to the children and to where the children, parents and other community members want it to be?
- How safe, easy and accessible are the routes between home, school, play spaces and other spaces?
- How easily can children and young people travel independently to outdoor play spaces in other areas?
- In spaces used by other groups and members of the community how well is 'shared use' negotiated and managed?
- What plans exist for the future development of land currently used by children and young people as outdoor play space?

Transport links to other areas may also be an important part of the picture, especially for older children and young people and in rural areas.

'I'd go to places if I could get a bus there or be taken or brought back.'
A 12-year-old boy

What plans exist for the development of local spaces?

There may be existing plans for developing or changing the local built environment. Hence any play audit should clarify what plans exist for public open spaces, dedicated play spaces and other open spaces. The local planning department should have this information.

Before any changes can be contemplated it is important to have a clear picture of capital and revenue expenditure, how this is distributed, which budgets it comes from and whether there is any commitment for it to continue. Account must also be taken of hidden costs such as management time, volunteers' hours and other resources.

Subjecting planning and development proposals relating to the outdoor environment to a 'play impact assessment' – an analysis of its potential impact on outdoor play – could highlight the effect potential changes might have on children and young people and ensure that their play needs are properly addressed as part of standard procedures.

Comparing supply and demand

After identifying existing supply and local needs, the next step is to compare supply and demand. This involves:

- identifying where needs of different groups of children and young people are currently being met;
- identifying where needs are not currently being met and the implications of this;
- establishing 'what works' now;
- identifying problems with existing provision;
- checking that children and young people with a wide range of needs and abilities will find any new developments both attractive and accessible.

The gaps might concern particular groups of the child population – perhaps older boys, older girls, children and young people from specific ethnic or religious groups, those who have identified specific needs or pre-school children. Or they might relate to types of play activity: access to wildlife spaces or facilities for skateboards, for example.

There are a number of reasons why disabled children do not use existing play spaces. For example, many playgrounds are inaccessible or have inaccessible equipment. In some areas playgrounds are in the middle of playing fields or recreation grounds, which can be difficult to cross, and safety surfaces such as sand or bark can be difficult to navigate.

Standards such as the Six Acre Standard (NPFA, 2001) may give some guidance about levels and standards of provision (see Chapter 4). However, they may not always be appropriate to local circumstances and are never a good substitute for local assessment of needs and wishes.

This BMX play track in Bristol is an alternative to hanging around on the streets and so helps young people to stay out. It also encourages them to take more exercise.

South Somerset works in partnership to meet the identified needs of young people

In South Somerset play provision has focused on the ubiquitous play area suitable for toddlers and young children. However, there were indications that the recreation needs of young people were not being met. So in 1999 the District Council made £80,000 available to support the development of appropriate informal recreation facilities for young people through grant aiding local groups.

Local groups were invited to express an interest in the project and as a result 12 asked to work in partnership with the District Council to develop facilities. The groups included parish councils, village hall committees and recreation trusts. During July 2000 council staff conducted a questionnaire-based survey of young people aged 8–16, surveying primary schools, secondary schools and youth clubs. A total of 1501 questionnaires were returned.

The questionnaire asked young people which facility they would most like to see in their parish and where they would like it to go. Examples were used to demonstrate of the types of facilities readily available, and the young people were free to suggest their own ideas. Results showed strong support for multi-use games areas, BMX play tracks, skating areas and youth shelters.

As well as consultation with the young people there have been open meetings, presentations and newsletter articles to involve the whole community. Where facilities need planning permission there will also be a statutory consultation process. The District Council is helping the 12 local groups to obtain quotations, identify additional sources of funding and make applications. The proposed facilities consist of 11 BMX play tracks, four multi-use games areas, three kick-about areas (a smaller version of a multi-use games area), five skating areas and three youth shelters. As a result of this project and the interest that it has generated, developing informal recreation facilities for young people is now a key issue in the District Council's Cultural Strategy.

2.6 Identifying funding

Key points in this section:

- A number of Government initiatives may provide funding
- Councils may also have access to funding through the planning process
- Funding will be needed for revenue and capital costs

A number of Government initiatives may provide funding

Many of the current Government initiatives described in Section 2.1 (pp. 19–22) are supported by dedicated funding that can be used to develop outdoor play space. For example, funding may be obtainable through Neighbourhood Renewal Strategies, the Children's Fund and a number of New Opportunities Fund Programmes (see also Chapter 4).

Councils may also have access to funding through the planning process

There may also be funds available through 'planning obligations', also known as 'Section 106' agreements. These are, typically, agreements between local planning authorities and developers negotiated in the context of granting a planning consent. They provide a means of ensuring that developers contribute towards the infrastructure and services that local authorities believe to be necessary to facilitate proposed developments. Contributions may either be in cash or in kind and are sometimes used for outdoor play provision. The Government has issued a consultation paper (DTLR, 2001d) setting out a new system in which the local authority's Local Plan sets out priorities for sustainable development and developers contribute on a tariff basis.

Funding will be needed for revenue and capital costs

However, much of this funding is either short term or aimed at capital expenditure. Problems can arise if there is not early agreement over continued funding for maintenance and development. Further information on funding sources for play provision can be obtained from the National Children's Bureau, Children's Play Information Service (see Useful organisations section, p.105).

3.1 General principles for successful outdoor play space

Key points in this section:

- Play spaces need to attract children and young people
- Location is probably the single most important success factor for outdoor play spaces
- Spaces need to feel secure
- Play spaces need to be accessible to all
- Well-maintained spaces help to attract children and young people

Play spaces need to attract children and young people

Some outdoor play spaces offer a wide variety of play opportunities. Others are very specific in what they offer. What matters in the degree of variety and choice within a neighbourhood. Good places to play actually attract children and young people because they can offer a quiet place to sit undisturbed by others, a place where they can look out for each other or a place where they can do whatever interests them at the time without worrying or being worried by adults. Play spaces often have strong cultural significance and children from different ethnic and cultural groups may be more attracted to play spaces if their differences are recognised and celebrated in those spaces.

Children and young people need to be able to play in the ways most suited to their own nature, interests and abilities, they need to be able to choose from the full range of play opportunities including:
- varied and interesting physical environments;
- physically challenging environments;
- natural elements – earth, water, fire, air;
- places for movement including running, jumping, rolling, climbing and balancing;
- places where they can manipulate natural and fabricated materials;
- experiences which stimulate their senses;
- places to experience change in the natural and built environment;
- opportunities for social interactions;
- opportunities to play with their identity;
- environments where they can experience a whole range of emotions.

Source: adapted from NPFA and others, 2000 (see also Hughes, 1996a)

Some outdoor play spaces may be better suited to some types of play than others but generally they are able to offer a wide range of opportunities if they are well thought out and designed (see Appendix 2). Play spaces must be stimulating, novel and contain an element of 'returnability'. Children should want to go back there over and over again. They should also be able to make their own games and play experiences from the facilities available to them.

3.1 General principles for successful outdoor play space

Location is probably the single most important success factor for outdoor play spaces

'On our way home from the playcentre we get harassed by dogs and boys.'
An Asian girl

In the right location, an average or even a poorly-designed space can be well used if not well valued. But a well-designed space, in the wrong place, is likely to fail. The key feature is the physical relationship between the space and the wider built environment that children spend time in. A good location will be:
- reasonably close to home;
- within sight of walking or cycling 'desire lines' or main travel routes;
- in spaces where there is 'informal oversight' from nearby houses or other well-used public spaces;
- in locations identified by children and young people as appropriate.

This means that play spaces are best located:
- at or near a busy entrance of a park, not a long way inside;
- in the middle of a housing estate, within view of the housing, not on the edge;
- near to other well used facilities such as shops, cafés and public transport.

The detailed location will vary depending on the target age group for the space. In some areas older young people may wish their spaces to be less 'overlooked' than younger children, while in others it might be important to locate spaces for older and younger children close together to allow older young people to watch over their younger friends or relatives. Decisions about location will often require compromises to be reached between different interest groups. For instance, some residents may resist the idea of recreational space near to their homes. A good participation process can help achieve these compromises. But if children's views about location are ignored in the face of adult opinion, there is a real risk that a space will fail.

> **Cuxton 'teenage village' shows the importance of location**
>
> In 1997 two 'teenage villages' were installed by the then Rochester upon Medway City Council. One of these was quickly vandalised and destroyed, while the other, in Cuxton, Rochester, is still well used. The site that was destroyed was located in a secluded urban area, while the successful site was in a rural area, overlooked and frequently visited.
>
> The teenage village in Cuxton is maintained by the parish council. The clerk of the parish council visits the site weekly, and the street sweepers keep it clean on a regular basis. The site itself requires little maintenance: it has three all-metal roundels linked by ramps made of logs that have been cut in half.

3.1 General principles for successful outdoor play space

But not all neighbourhoods are attractive to children and young people and in many areas they feel marginalised. Neighbourhoods may display signs designed and placed by adults in an attempt to protect themselves, their property and their peace and quiet. While signs that say 'no ball games', 'no cycling' or 'no skating' may express valid adult perspectives and needs, they not only take away some of the few places children and young people have to play but also tell them their normal childhood activities are not wanted in the area.

'Children may play here' sign, Stirling

Stirling Council publicly acknowledges children's right to use public spaces

Stirling Council in Scotland devised a 'Children may play here' sign to emphasise to children and young people that they are welcome to play in public open spaces. The signs are used in unequipped, informal spaces as well as in equipped areas that are obviously for children. The Council also avoids using negative signs stopping children from playing except in exceptional circumstances.

Spaces need to feel secure

If children and young people do not feel secure in a play environment they will not use it. Personal safety is an important factor in the amount of time children and young people play outside. Their fears and those of their parents often prevent them from going to places that might offer them excellent play opportunities. Fear of bullying by other children and young people and their parents' fears of strangers are two of the most powerful influences (Children's Play Council and the Children's Society, 2001; Child Accident Prevention Trust, 2001).

Surveys show that parents are very concerned that their children maybe harmed by strangers, and children are also worried. These fears are reinforced by media coverage of abductions, police investigations and court cases. In the face of these fears, it is important to keep the risks in perspective. However, the growth in fear in recent years is not based on any increase in the real risks children face. Children are no more likely to be abducted today than their parents or grandparents were when they were young.

In some spaces, increased supervision may be an appropriate response to these anxieties. Neighbourhood and street wardens and park rangers can have an important role in persuading parents and children that outdoor play spaces are safe for them to use. However, these people need to like and communicate well with children and young people and understand their outdoor play needs.

But often, practical improvements to play space can help reduce the level of fear. Improvements that increase the level of use of public spaces in cities have in the past been shown to lead people to feel safer through 'safety in numbers' (Whyte, 1980), and this is likely to be the case with play spaces.

A sense of community ownership is also important in security. Where people have been actively involved in planning and developing open spaces in their neighbourhoods they are more likely to have met each other and felt that the upkeep and safety of the area is a priority. People who have had provision imposed on them without any discussion about their views and needs are not likely to care about the safety or security of the facility.

O'Brien and others (2000) found that children themselves had many concerns about safety issues in the local urban spaces. About one third of the children were anxious about unsafe places in their own neighbourhoods and slightly more were concerned about unknown young people and adults. In inner London the children were more concerned about the safety of their streets, and dark and dingy places were universally disliked. In a new town children found poorly lit underpasses, which were actually there to help them cross roads, very frightening. Children living in social housing estates found lifts and stairways frightening.

Although younger children and their parents may feel reassured by the presence of park staff, young people often feel they encroach on their free use of the park. Park staff must be properly trained, like and understand the needs of young people and be able to make judgements about the behaviour of young people. They need to be able to distinguish between behaviour that is merely uncomfortable for others because of their own prejudices, and behaviour that is truly anti-social or criminal. Respect for the right of children and young people to use the space for their own enjoyment is an important element in the management of public open spaces.

Face painting fun at a Reccy Roadshow
Photo by The Children's Team

Cambridge: knowing staff are available helps children feel safer

Recreation Rangers ('Reccy Rangers') were set up in the city of Cambridge in 1997, with two rangers working six to eight hours a week. Their brief is threefold: to promote the use of recreation grounds by the whole community; to provide safe play opportunities for children and young people; and to monitor site maintenance. Today there are six rangers working up to 25 hours a week, promoting safe use of recreation areas with an emphasis on play. As a result of the success of the initiative a further two rangers are due to be employed in 2002.

Rangers are predominately based within areas of greatest need. They have their own area of the city, which they get to know intimately by visiting local residents' associations, regularly attending local meetings, and being very visible within the community. Each Ranger has a bright red T-shirt and spends a lot of time within the local parks and recreation ground. Within the parks they run play activities and 'Reccy Roadshows'.

Some examples of their work are:
- community pantomime;
- community film;
- play days;
- twilight play activities in the summer.

The rangers are trained play workers. For many local residents they are the first point of contact with the council. It is a high profile position that lends a very positive image of the council to the residents of Cambridge.

Local authority child protection guidelines and policies might need to incorporate children's and young people's outdoor play. All staff who regularly come into contact with children and young people, either formally or informally, should be covered by standard child protection procedures.

Proposals put forward by the NSPCC for making parks safer include:
- improved supervision – the presence of park keepers and rangers;
- better lighting;
- age-appropriate play areas;
- signs prohibiting adults entering unless they are with children;
- better fencing around play areas;
- telephones nearby;

- improved toilet facilities;
- traffic calming and reduction in and around the park;
- improved play facilities;
- more opportunities for young people in parks;
- regular safety audits.

Source: Sexty, 2000

Play spaces need to be accessible to all

If children cannot get to play spaces easily and without being afraid of what might happen to them either on the way or whilst there, they are not going to use them. Play spaces on or near busy roads are not popular; neither are those that involve crossing busy roads or using dark, hidden paths. Access is an issue for all children and young people, but especially for those with disabilities, so their active involvement in development projects is crucial.

Merely creating physical accessibility may not be sufficient to ensure that disabled and non-disabled children and young people are able to play together and meet the needs of others with minority needs and interests for outdoor play space. If children and young people are not used to playing out, they are unlikely to start unless they are told about changes that have been made, and positively attracted and made to feel welcome. Parents and carers will also need to be convinced that their children will be welcomed and safe when playing out, as this may be a new experience for them, too. Provision of one-to-one support may be necessary to enable severely disabled children to access play space (Scott, 2000).

Educating children and young people in road safety procedures, while important, is only a small part of protecting them from road danger. One of the most important methods of improving access to outdoor play space is by introducing traffic-controlling measures. If children and young people are to be safe when playing out, their needs should be given proper attention in residential areas and on routes to known play spaces.

Traffic and highways engineers need to be knowledgeable about the places where children move around and play. They should ensure that traffic speeds are controlled in the appropriate areas, crossings are sited on the routes children use and in places where they will be used, and footpaths, cycle tracks and pavements along children's routes are well lit and properly maintained.

In the last 20 years, the number of cars has risen by 80 per cent. The car now dominates the local places where children could once play safely with their friends within earshot of their homes. In 2000 nearly 80 per cent of the 3593 children and young people between five and 15 who were killed or seriously injured in road accidents, were either pedestrians or riding their bikes (DTLR, 2001a).

Matthews and others (1998) found that many young people were uncomfortable when out on their own in the streets but felt safer with their friends. Comments about fear of traffic were common. Safe streets were felt to be those close to home or relatives, away from traffic, where there were other people around and where young people were not bothered by others.

Ealing improves safe access through traffic management

SALSA (Sustainable Access to Leisure Sites and Amenities), a project based in Ealing, West London, aims to create safer routes to play and recreation facilities. Funded by the European Life Environment Programme, it aimed to extend the 'safe routes to school' concept to play centres, parks, sports centres, swimming pools and libraries. In 2000 SALSA built four new routes for pedestrians and cyclists. Aimed specifically at children, the routes linked estates and residential neighbourhoods with local parks, swimming pools, play centres, youth centres and other leisure facilities.

Behind the initiative lay concerns about children's and young people's increasing reliance on parents to transport them to activities. Research showed that escorted journeys to leisure facilities were most often made by car and involved very short distances. Children dependent on adults to take part in leisure activities were often getting less exercise then they needed and were participating in active leisure pastimes less often than they would like to.

The publicity generated by the project was intended to encourage children to try the routes over the school summer holidays. It was also hoped that clear, sensible information about safety would help give parents the confidence to give their children more independence and freedom. A competition sponsored by Raleigh (permanent notice boards at destinations, posters and information packs handed out to every child aged 10–12) helped to promote the project.

Consultations with local parents identified the most wanted road improvements in their area and ultimately these were the essential components of the complete route in each of the four areas. Improvements included seven zebra crossings and two

Using a safe route to leisure facilities

The Mayor of Ealing, Cllr Philip Portwood, showing the way in cycling to leisure facilities

toucan (pedestrian-controlled) crossings, eight raised junctions, nine traffic calming schemes, eight refuge crossing points, four side junction treatments, three lighting schemes, 4km of new cycle lanes safe from traffic and a CCTV scheme.

As well as these road improvements in each area, secure cycle parking has been provided at 21 leisure facilities and a pilot scheme allowed cycling through Acton Park. The scheme is managed by the park's rangers service and signage is used to advise cyclists that pedestrians have priority and they should maintain slow cycle speeds.

Ealing Council committed over £750,000 to the project and the European Life Environment programme grant totalled £417,000. There were other contributions in terms of time and support from the partner organisations.

Further information about the project may be found at www.ealing.gov.uk/salsa.

Well maintained spaces help to attract children and young people

'There is nothing to play on and the playground is covered in glass. People use it to take drugs.'

Large numbers of children's playgrounds, whether in parks and other green spaces or in other areas, are poorly maintained and dirty. Children and young people are keenly aware of the state of the playgrounds they use and understand the messages this gives about the attitudes of adults to play spaces. Dog fouling is a major concern for children and parents – and a health risk. Experience suggests that properly enforced fines may tackle the problem more efficiently than special dog mess bins.

In the NSPCC study fewer than half the play areas in parks were described as 'clean' and fewer than half were described as 'well-maintained'. Only one in five were considered to have adequate lighting, one in three had toilets nearby and 28 per cent had telephones within reach. Only a third of the adults thought the play area was safe and two-thirds thought it could be made safer (Sexty, 2000).

Young people are also concerned about the lack of maintenance in many parks and other green spaces. Those who take their younger brothers and sisters to parks are keenly aware of the dangers of broken glass and poorly maintained play equipment (Greenhalgh and Worpole, 1995).

Bradford City Council tackles the issue of dog mess

In 1998 Bradford Council took up designated powers under the Dogs (Fouling of Land) Act 1996. Under the Act the responsibility for the removal of dog faeces clearly became that of the owner, with £25 fixed penalty fines for offences, or up to £1000 if the case was successfully taken to court. The Council decided that rather than spending money on what it considered to be the owners' responsibility, it would redirect the monies to increase the number of the park rangers, who would become authorised to enforce the Act, issuing fixed penalty tickets across the district.

The Council removed bins from all 17 'poop scoop' sites and relied instead on sustained enforcement of the new Act. The first ticket was issued in June 1998 and between then and January 2002, 457 fixed penalty tickets had been issued at locations across the district with over 90 per cent of the fines being paid either voluntarily or through the courts. The legislation appears to be working, making the Council's open spaces cleaner and more readily usable, especially by small children.

3.2 Essential design principles of a good play environment

Key points in this section:

■ Children need both simple and complex environments to play in
■ Stimulating environments require creative design
■ There is no one way to produce an ideal play space
■ Play spaces are for everyone

Children need both simple and complex environments to play in

'Each and every playground should be designed as if it is unique in that it has a unique geographical setting and population. The character, and perhaps history, of the area, should be reflected in the spaces, in the landscaping and in the furniture. Dramatic or prevailing natural features should be included.'
Hendricks, 2001

Children and young people get the best play experiences if they can choose from a variety of activities and have access to equipment and environments that are able to be manipulated. Simple structures, for example, slides, swings or see-saws have one obvious use and encourage one type of activity with few opportunities for the children to improvise or manipulate the units. Complex environments may include these simple structures but also have additional elements including, for example, water and sand, different heights and levels, natural and built features, and fixed and moveable items. These more complex environments allow children and young people to be more imaginative in the way they play; when an area contains more than one type of material it allows children many more choices for manipulating the resources and ways of playing (Stine, 1997).

Water features – fountains, paddling pools, lakes and ponds – are very popular. On warm (and even not so warm) days children and young people can get hours of pleasure running in and out of well-designed fountains, as shown by the popularity of public spaces such as Somerset House in London or Sheffield's Peace Garden.

Stimulating environments require creative design

The aim of design is to put ideas and goals into reality and to make sense of a space by giving it meaning. A good park or play space will lift the spirits of visitors. Designers of play spaces help to raise expectations and broaden horizons. They challenge the commonplace off-the-shelf solution. They ensure that participation is complemented by inspiration.

Planning, developing and designing children's and young people's outdoor play spaces requires imagination and the understanding that:
■ children do not always do what adults expect of them;

Sheffield Peace Garden. Photo by ID8 photography

'Designing for play should be seen as an art form – like composing music, writing a new stage play or creating a new painting … Good art for children must touch and communicate to the children and good design in children's play spaces would be designs that communicate some insight into life on this planet and some elements of playfulness in a way that children perceive and appreciate the message in the design.'
Hendricks, 2001

- the children of today are not the children of tomorrow;
- children and young people grow up and their interests change;
- children's dynamics and their relationships with adults and each other frequently change as they explore attitudes and emotions;
- children are seduced by and follow fashions in the same way as adults.

Design must therefore create play spaces with the potential for change and flexibility. A major problem is that designers are often not used at all (parks or commissioning staff with no access to play expertise may simply repeat what they have done before) or are brought in at too late a stage in the process.

Although children's and young people's play fashions and interests change, the basic types of outdoor play are fairly constant. Play spaces that offer sufficient and in-built flexibility are likely to be used for most new play interests with only minor modifications. Keeping abreast of what local children and young people are doing and needing through continuous dialogue and participation will help play providers keep up with play fashions and trends.

Hounslow listens to children

The old playground in Redless Park, Isleworth in the London Borough of Hounslow was situated on a mature putting green with mature trees, bushes and shrub planting. The play equipment had to be demolished and shut due to Health and Safety risks. New funds were secured from the Capital Challenge programme to build a new playground.

The play in the community team and the landscape design team consulted with local children to find out what they wanted to see and what they enjoyed most about the old playground. The children said the thing they enjoyed most about the old playground was the trees, bushes and the shrubs and planting. They loved hiding; chasing and playing hide and seek games.

A new design based on the children's ideas planned to keep all of the natural play elements they so enjoyed. The Metropolitan Police Crime Prevention Officer was then invited to give their view on the design proposals. The police were worried about the number of gates and entrances as they were concerned that if they were chasing someone lots of exits made their job difficult. It was explained that more exits made it easier for children to avoid bullying and any other dangerous incidents.

The Police also wanted all the shrubs and bushes to be removed so they could see into the playground. It was explained that the children loved the bushes and that they were part of the playground. Slightly reluctantly the police accepted this. The bushes were reduced in height but none were removed. The children got what they wanted and also a new playground, which they greatly enjoy.

There is no one way to produce an ideal play space

Planners and designers need to think in terms of the potential for different types of activity and play opportunity rather than in term of specific pieces of equipment. The different ways in which children and young people play are outlined in Appendix 2.

Three writers on play space design have developed and published useful guides to the practicalities of developing children's play spaces. Each have listed the criteria they feel important.

Criteria for a good outdoor play space:
■ Attractive and secure: to both adults and children.
■ Access and movement: space and flow which allows children to walk, run, use wheelchairs and other mobility aids, ride bikes and skate. Consideration needs to be given to the separation of foot and bike paths as combined spaces can be very difficult for people who have visual and hearing difficulties.
■ Opportunities for challenge and risk taking: children of different ages and with differing levels of physical ability and confidence should all be able to do activities which physically and mentally stretch and challenge them.
■ Minimal unexpected hazards: hidden hazards such as buried glass or poorly maintained equipment are more dangerous than equipment and spaces where the potential risks are easily visible and obvious.
■ Provision for the wide range of interests and abilities of children by using a variety of materials and natural forms, and a mixture of simple, single-use features and other more complex ones which allow children to use their imagination and creativity.
■ Moveable parts that can be changed or moved around by the children to increase the different ways in which they can play.
■ Places where adults can watch or relax while the children play.
■ Variety of multi-sensory materials and forms which create smells, noises, different textures and contrasting colours and shades.
■ Clear divisions of space that make it clear for whom the space is intended and the type of activities which might be best performed there. Spaces of different sizes and with

3.2 Essential design principles of a good play environment

Enjoying time with friends at the Adventure Zone, North Hull Adventure Playground

different texture, contours and structures or planting.
- Clear, easy to read signs, at a height children can read, stating any specific purposes for which a space is recommended.
- Safety: well maintained equipment and surfacing suitable for the use and misuse of the equipment.

Source: adapted from Hart, 1993

When used as an analytical tool by designers, these nine pairs of design elements help to widen the vision for children's play, and clarify what is missing as well as what already exists.

Accessible	Inaccessible
Active	Passive
Challenge and risk	Repetition and security
Hard	Soft
Natural	Manufactured
Open	Closed
Permanence	Changes
Private	Public
Simple	Complex

Source: Stine, 1997

Characteristics of successful public playgrounds:
- areas large enough to divide up into different types of space including large open spaces and smaller enclosed spaces;
- areas which are sunny and shaded;
- areas where children can experiences different textures, sounds, smells, shapes forms and colours and tastes;
- easily recognisable by children as a place primarily for them to play;
- the space invites children to explore the area, looking for new and different experiences;
- the space offers opportunities for different physical actions such as swinging, rocking, climbing, sliding, rolling, jumping, running;
- there are curving lines, flowing, waving or snake-like forms,

as well as straighter forms and bars more attractive to an adult's perception;
- places where adults can see and be seen but are not intruding on the children's spaces;
- variations in the ground elevation and texture;
- good hiding and 'secret' places.

Source: adapted from Hendricks, 2001

Play spaces are for everyone

The Disability Discrimination Act 1995 requires that those providing children's play spaces do not discriminate against disabled children. By 2004 service providers must have made 'reasonable adjustments' to physical features of their premises to overcome barriers to access and this has implications for all those responsible for neighbourhood environments.

The first step in making playgrounds accessible is consultation with disability organisations, disabled children and parents. This does not mean that a playground can be adapted for every need or that every piece of equipment will be suitable for all disabled children, rather that as many physical and sensory impairments are taken on to account as possible (Scott, 2000).

Low cost solutions and simple changes to play areas can make a significant difference to their accessibility for disabled children and young people. There are many access and design features that could easily be incorporated into play areas to make them more inclusive. Some access and design points that can be incorporated include:
- paths that are wide and clearly marked;
- safety tiles or 'wet pour' provide more accessible surfaces;
- handrails fitted to all ramps and steps leading to equipment enable children with mobility difficulties to use them independently;
- bright colours, different textures and sounds help children with visual difficulties identify objects and distinguish different areas within the playground;
- many standard low-level crawling and climbing nets, tunnels and tubes can be accessed and explored by children with quite severe mobility difficulties;
- special swing seats designed for physically disabled children can also be incorporated;
- 'adventure trails' can make a useful contribution to play experiences for children who are physically disabled.

Source: Children's Play Council, Kidsactive and Mencap, 2002
Based on material from Action for Leisure

It's fun to be spooky – Halloween celebrations at North Hull Adventure Playground

The wheelchair swing, very much a favourite with wheelchair users

North Hull Adventure Playground is an inclusive play environment

Since its inception the site at the North Hull Adventure Playground has been designed to allow children of all abilities to make full use of the facilities. The whole site is wheelchair accessible and there is specialised equipment, including a wheelchair swing and roundabout, a soft playroom and a changing room that includes sensory equipment.

The playground provides a short break care scheme for the children of 25 families in the city of Kingston upon Hull and surrounding areas in the East Riding of Yorkshire. Initially funding was secured from social services and the local health authority to provide four workers to give one-to-one support for children with additional needs during the school holidays. In 2001 new funding was made available to extend the scheme to after-school club hours and on Saturdays throughout the year.

Children are able to join in with all of the activities on the site because of the extra support they are given, combating feelings of exclusion and giving the children and their families some respite and relief. The scheme receives far more requests than it can currently accommodate.

Rhythm and music workshop

3.3 A menu of dedicated play spaces

Good outdoor play opportunities for children and young people of different ages will involve a mix of facilities specially built for them, including:

- playgrounds;
- skateboard and skate parks;
- bike tracks and jumps;
- hangout or youth shelters;
- adventure playgrounds;
- other open access play projects;
- city farms, woodland spaces and nature reserves;
- multi-use games areas;
- fun trails and activity courses;
- school playgrounds.

Playgrounds

Children helping create Camden Street playground in Walsall

Adults perceive playgrounds as small areas of land with standard playground equipment to be used in a prescribed way. Children's perceptions are different. They expect less stereotyped play equipment, which signals that the space is 'for them', a kind of sign that says 'Play here – children and children's play are important!'. Play equipment not only offers the opportunity to swing, jump, slide and bounce about, it also provides an important social focus regardless of its style or appearance. It offers a place where children can gather with their friends and do things that they might not have an opportunity to do elsewhere. The way children use equipment in playgrounds is not always the way it is intended and allowance must be made for this in design and installation. Testing out different ways in which equipment can be used and inventing new ones is an important and natural part of children's development and exploration. Playground equipment should be suitable for the age of the children and young people for whom it is intended and accessible to those who have mobility difficulties.

The presence of play equipment may be one reason why children go to parks or to playgrounds, but once there they may get involved in other sorts of play activities. The location and character of the landscape surrounding each playground or equipment area is just as important as the design of the equipment itself.

Well-used playgrounds are an important meeting place for parents and carers as well as children. Improved physical access to these sites benefits whole families and supports the increasing independence of children and young people.

Bole Hill Playground before rebuilding

Bole Hill Playground after rebuilding
Both photos by Sheffield City Council

Sheffield Bole Hill Recreation Ground: residents tackle a run-down playground

The playground at Bole Hill Recreation Ground in Sheffield had been deteriorating over many years. Much of the play equipment had been removed having been deemed unsafe. Eventually, local residents got together and formed a Friends' Group to address the problems of the playground within their local park.

They set about various local fundraising projects to raise money for new equipment in the park, obtaining over £100,000 from the National Lottery with the Council's assistance. The Council created a detailed 10-year lease agreement with the Friends for the playground, and the Friends and local people selected equipment and designs from several suppliers. This included a space-net, swings, see-saw, toddler multi-unit, spring equipment, five-a-side goals and various other pieces. The playground was also fenced off from the remainder of the park to stop dogs gaining entry. The refurbishment was completed in the summer of 1999.

The Council maintain the playground for the group and also carry the liability for any problems. The Friends help to keep the playground clear of litter and graffiti and have been involved with local children and park rangers in the planting of shrubs, flowers and bulbs and the installation of seats and picnic tables. An annual independent playground area assessor rated the playground second in play value amongst the 175 playgrounds of the City of Sheffield.

A second park in Sheffield, Blackbrook Road Playing Fields, has since obtained £139,000 of National Lottery funding for its playground, and the Council have leased the area to a local group.

Leicester Eastleigh Road Play Area: creating and maintaining a small new space

The Eastleigh Road play area is relatively small and is situated within a densely populated region of the City. It was developed in 1994 in response to a lack of play space for children under seven years old in the area, at a cost of £57,000. The site is only 200 square metres and it is enclosed on three sides by walls more than 2.5 metres in height. The site was developed to be attractive to adults as well as children as there are few private gardens in the area.

The design incorporated play equipment within a landscaped environment that placed great emphasis on providing climbing and scented shrubs. In order to provide a wide range of play experiences in such a confined space, static rather than mobile play features were selected. To enhance play value they were carefully chosen and sand was used to be both the predominant surface and an integral play component. All equipment was

Eastleigh Road Play Area – view from street entrance

chosen to encourage social and imaginative play and allow adults watching over the children to participate to a high degree.

The local residents, who were closely consulted in the developmental process, were given keys to the site. Unfortunately a few problems arose because of the transient nature of the local population, but employing wardens to lock and unlock the facility solved this. Another problem involved late night drinkers and graffiti, which has been dealt with by the wardens and by raising the height of the fences at the entrance to the site to stop late-night entry.

Fixed play equipment has always been an important element in children's and young people's outdoor play opportunities. Although, like most people, children and young people are often keen on purchasing new equipment and enjoy 'shopping' from glossy catalogues with designers, simple resources can also provide a wide range of play opportunities.

Ordinary items and features can make interesting play areas

Resource	Use
Old car tyres	Use to used to mark out tracks, make swinging walkways, tunnels, steps, leap-frogs, dragons, seats and benches; piled up on central stakes and filled with clean sand to make mountains and heaps for climbing and hung up to make different types of swings
Ropes	Ladders, swings and bridges
Tunnels, mounds and other landscaping	Use for exciting play
Tarmac areas	Make more interesting with surface markings
Flat grass surfaces	Good for running, ball games, sitting or lying quietly
Hard edging and low walls	Good for skateboard and rollerblade manoeuvres, sitting chatting, balancing, playing with small cars and toys or, for small children, jumping off

Sand	Popular as a place to sit, to dig, to build, to bury, to sift, to sort and to mix with water
Shrubs	Good places to hide, tunnel, sit quietly, find small animals and insects, discover natural textures and smells, find materials for building and pretend play, finding brightly coloured and beautiful shapes and flowers
Rocks	Good for building and dam making
Trees with low branches	Good to climb and swing from

Play equipment is rarely just used for the original design purpose. A key element of design, therefore, is to make sure that the item or facility is robust, that it can be used in a variety of ways and that attempts are made to ensure that such use is unlikely to result in injury to the child or young person.

Features designed for by adults may be used in different ways by children

Feature	Use
Paths	For hop-scotch, cycling, skating, bouncing balls, skipping, running and hopping
Pergolas	For swinging on, hanging ropes, climbing, perching on the top and using as goal posts
Walls	For walking along, climbing up, jumping off, sitting on, hiding behind, and roller-blade and skateboard tricks
Gates	For swinging from, climbing over and vaulting
Bollards	For leapfrog, balancing, jumping over
Slides	For running up
Bouncy 'animals' and shapes	For seeing how hard and high you can get before falling off

Tyre swings	For sitting chatting or seeing how many people will fit on
Low branches and bushes	For dens, hideouts, quiet corners and spaces with a degree of seclusion

Skateboard and skating parks

The use of skateboards and skates is particularly popular with boys who often seek out areas where there are smooth hard surfaces with short steep slopes, humps, curbs, steps and walls to hone and develop their skills and tricks. Children and young people often find that the places offering the most challenging and interesting 'courses' for these activities are in areas designed for general use by the public and that their opportunities are restricted. In response to this a number of local authorities have worked with children and young people to identify suitable site for these activities and to develop and build skateboard and skating parks which meet the physically challenging needs of these highly skilled activities.

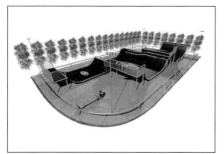

Artist's impression of Nuneaton Skate Park

'Skate Park Jam' at Bedworth Skate Park

'Big Air' at Bedworth Skate Park

Nuneaton and Bedworth Council creates two skateboard and skating parks

In late 2000 Nuneaton and Bedworth Council announced that they were to build two skate facilities in the local area: a street complex in Bedworth and a more 'extreme' ramp complex in Nuneaton (for full details of the facilities visit the website www.nuneatonandbedworthskateparks.com). An elected committee of young people manages the parks.

The opening of the parks was marked by an 'opening jam' held at both sites. Local bands and DJs performed along with graffiti demonstrations and fun for all the family. This led to another jam at the end of summer with more music, a skateboard competition and international graffiti artist 'Shok 1' painting an anti-drugs mural in Bedworth, which is still there today. The outdoor parks are open seven days a week, free of charge and are flood-lit until 9.30pm.

Tribe Enterprises supports skate park developments

Tribe Enterprises is a non-profit making organisation that develops skate facilities for young people, providing mobile skate parks, after-school clubs and independent advice on wheeled sports. As part of Tribe's commitment to developing the sport in younger children, it runs after-school clubs for 8's to 14's. These clubs not only provide a safe environment for less experienced skaters to practice and improve, but also offer one-to-one tuition. At Tribe's local club in Maidenhead, around 100 skaters attend every Tuesday evening at the local leisure centre.

Another area of Tribe's work is offering consultancy to councils and local authorities. There are three main stages in this process. First they meet the local authority and discuss the issues behind constructing a skate park (location, safety, promotion etc.). The council then funds a test event, which involves a mobile skate facility, with the intention of gauging local interest. All the skaters that attend these days are given questionnaires that provide Tribe with a broader picture of the needs of the local skaters. Any members of the local community that are watching the event are also asked to fill in a questionnaire so that their opinion can also be taken into account. Tribe then uses this information to help the local authority to design, install and manage a skate park. Tribe will also run a launch event with professional skaters, music competitions etc. when the park is ready to open. Tribe also hires out mobile skate parks for one-off events.

Bike tracks and jumps

Although the design requirements of bike tracks and jumps may be similar to those of skateboard and skating parks, they are not always the same. The main excitement for many young bike riders is to go fast and be increasingly daring in the tricks and feats they perform. They need space, surfaces and contours that allow them to pick up speed, jump and spin their bikes land safely and continue moving at speed. Bike tracks frequently have rougher surfaces than skating parks.

BMX play tracks allow young people to have fun riding their bikes off road on a purpose-built and maintainable facility

South Somerset creates BMX tracks

Dirt BMX tracks were clearly found, in South Somerset, to be the most desired type of BMX track. This was because of the high number of young people in the area with mountain bikes/BMX bikes who just wanted somewhere informal and safe (non-concrete) to simply turn up and ride.

Youth shelters

Young people want places where they can sit and talk, sometimes privately, sometimes in the view of other young people involved in other activities. Most young people do not want to disturb or be disturbed by adults but frequently they have nowhere to go other than busy public areas. Youth or hangout shelters are becoming increasing popular as places for young people to meet and socialise. These shelters offer a covered seated area, designed and located in such a way as to make it clear to everyone that these are spaces for specifically for the use of young people.

In 1999 Thames Valley Police published a guide on developing youth shelters and sports systems (Hampshire and Wilkinson, 1999). In showing how useful many young people had found the recently

installed facilities, the authors of the guide were keen to point out that in order for them to be successful it was crucial to:
- identify local problems and issues first;
- ensure it was what local young people wanted;
- make sure that the nearest residents would not object.

The authors state that the shelter may not be the most important product of the project: the process of involvement, and that empowerment and training may do more for the young people involved than the shelter itself.

Two examples of youth shelters

Oxfordshire leads the way with youth shelters

Youth shelters were first installed in Oxfordshire in the late 1990s. Since then a number have been built. Initially, discussions were held with local community groups to promote the benefits of youth shelters to the area for young people. Once constructed it was found that the least successful were those that were hidden away. The shelters that were close to amenities, visible and most successful are either near or form part of a sporting facility. In Oxford City they have combined sport and youth shelters into 'street sport' sites, which can cost up to £30,000 per site. In Witney a youth shelter has been placed outside a parade of shops. The cost of youth shelters starts at £1500.

Adventure playgrounds

Adventure playgrounds are open access play spaces staffed by skilled playworkers. They are usually sited in residential areas and are often popular play places for children who have access to a wide range of indoor and outdoor facilities and resources. Parents know their children are being supervised by skilled staff who understand children's and young people's needs and aspirations. The essence of adventure playgrounds is that they are places that children can actively help create and shape the play environment, have opportunities for adventurous play, and take risks in a supported environment.

Adventure playgrounds sited in accessible locations are often better used than unstaffed play areas close to home. Many children and young people who use adventure playgrounds regularly spend much of their spare time there because they are able to come and go as they please (or as instructed by their parents). Others arrive for short periods and come and go throughout the day, picking and choosing what they will do and when they will leave. There are seasonal variations in attendance, demonstrating that the playgrounds are meeting a range of different needs.

Stamshaw Adventure Playground offers access to the elements in a fun way

Adventure playgrounds can accommodate many types of play, including rough and tumble – shown here in play fighting at Stamshaw Adventure Playground

Stamshaw Adventure Playground: a staffed play environment

Portsmouth City Council's play policy, written by the play service with PLAYLINK, recognises the need for specific and specialist play provision, such as adventure playgrounds. The policy also acknowledges that the role of the playworker is critical to achieving a safe, stimulating and rich play environment. Playworkers are a resource for children: supportive adults who do not unnecessarily interfere with or lead a child's play, but who are there to be called upon when required.

Stamshaw Adventure Playground is one of four full-time play sites entirely funded by Portsmouth City Council. It is a 3000 metre-square site situated in a park that also contains a floodlit football area controlled by the playground, and a fixed equipment play area that is maintained by another department of the City Council. The playground was built in 1981 and has been an integral part of the community ever since. Children can come and go as they please and there is no admission charge.

Stamshaw Adventure Playground costs £86,000 per year to run and employs three full time staff as well as sessional workers. It is open five days a week throughout the year and seven days a week during the summer holidays. Children from all over the city use the playground with attendance varying between 20 and 170 children a day depending on the time of year and the weather.

Some children and young people come for specific activities. Some spend many hours there, some just come and wait for their friends before going on. Sometimes children using the playground come in because of trouble outside or for first aid. Most are regular visitors from the local community and come for many years; some are second-generation children and some even become playworkers.

In addition to the activities normally provided by the playground, staff provide support and a distant eye for the young people who hang around in the park. This has developed into staffing an intermediate project at the nearby leisure centre. Staff occasionally support a local school with help for victims of bullying. This project operates from the playground after the open access session and staff are also closely involved with other agencies in providing support for children with a variety of needs.

Open access play projects

In some areas there are staffed play projects, either on fixed sites or run from mobile projects such as play buses, open to children and young people to come and go as they please, but which do not necessarily provide as wide a range of play opportunities as adventure playgrounds. Where these are sited close to residential areas and offer a sufficient range of opportunities and activities they, too, are popular with children and young people.

> **Bognor Fun Bus: a mobile play project**
>
> Bognor Fun Bus provides mobile open access play services for children aged five and above who live in and around Bognor Regis, West Sussex. It provides a broad range of activities for local children, including a neighbourhood play programme at 10 sites for two-month periods (two sessions per week); summer programmes at 12 sites; a half-term playscheme (at a fixed site); a Christmas arts scheme and a Saturday club on an estate.

City farms, woodland spaces and nature reserves

From plan to action – building play spaces in Brentor, Devon

City farms, managed spaces in woodland and nature reserves can offer children and young people opportunities and experiences they can get nowhere else. Creative approaches can be taken to providing play opportunities based on the nature of the space. Although many of the activities taking place in these environments have specific functions, for example, feeding and caring for animals or plants, they frequently allow participants to decide if and how they will take part and there is little or no coercion involved.

> **Heeley City Farm, Sheffield: a participative regeneration project**
>
> Heeley City Farm in Sheffield is a community-based and led youth, training and employment project in the inner city. The city farm model has been used to create a regeneration enterprise based on the management of a highly valued green space. The farm has a high level of participation as it has play facilities, interesting animal attractions, a café and a garden centre to attract visitors.

Multi-use games areas (MUGAs)

These areas often consist of flat, hard, surfaces surrounded by 'see-through' fencing and can include goal posts, hoops and nets for ad hoc ball games and informal practice. They are often popular with young people looking for semi-sporting activities and places to gather and socialise.

Fun trails and activity courses

These 'courses' are becoming increasingly popular and can offer children different types of play experience. They tend to be constructed primarily of wood with hoops, ropes, beams nets, metal poles, ladders and slopes.

School playgrounds

In some areas school playgrounds may be the only dedicated play spaces children and young people have access to. But they may not be open when the school is closed. In a few areas, schools are beginning to look at ways in which they can serve the local community more widely. Opening their playgrounds and outdoor spaces to children during out-of-school hours is one way to do this. However, management, maintenance and insurance issues can prove difficult to resolve and need careful investigation before shared use can be realised.

3.4 Creating and improving other places where children and young people play

Outdoor play opportunities can be increased by making improvements to spaces that have wider uses, such as:
- Parks, playing fields, green spaces and commons
- Residential streets
- Other open public spaces

Parks, playing fields, green spaces and commons

A park is a place 'to grow up in – you go through every stage in the park'
A young person, quoted in Greenhalgh and Worpole, 1995.

Although parks, playing fields and other green spaces often contain playgrounds they are important places for play in their own right. Good parks offer younger children, especially in urban areas, freedom and a play space away from traffic. The green spaces, trees, plants and small animals found in parks may be the only regular access city children have to the natural environment. Parks frequently have other features attractive to children for play. These include informal sports facilities, ponds and paddling pools, fountains, hills and slopes, smooth paths and surfaces, steps, walls, bandstands, sculptures, pergolas and bridges. Parks are also full of natural playthings such as trees, hills, shrubs, hollows, hedges, wide-open, flat green spaces, and a whole range of different surface textures.

Tunstall Park (described by Robin Moore) shows how parks can provide wonderful play spaces for children. In this park, an amazing variety of structures and built forms were interwoven. There were opportunities for children to look at wildlife, for example, dragonflies and goldfish, there were built structures, for example, a castle which appeared to have no purpose except as an architectural folly. There were large stone-retaining walls topped with a heavy balustrade jutting out to a steep, grassy slope. It was possible to climb the slope to where the castle floor was level with the ground and to then to walk around the balustrade. Children played hide-and-seek and war chase games there, watched for birds in the treetops, swung on ropes and played numerous games. Falling leaves could be thrown and rolled in, and grassy banks were there to be run up and rolled down. There were places where children could copy and pretend to be statues, and places to sit quietly and talk. Bushy areas offered opportunities for creating small dens and hideouts and for making tunnels within the trees. Water in the park was also important and there was a lake with boats for hire (Moore, 1990).

Children's thoughts about how parks could be more attractive to them and their peers tend to be about the whole park and not just the playgrounds. In one survey in the mid-1990s children said they would like to have more adventurous equipment for abseiling, rope walks, soft landings, assault courses and bike tracks as well as quiet places such as mazes, garden ponds and places to worship. They also were interested in getting more involved in the life of the park, especially through events such as music bands, festivals, managing wildlife areas and having the chance to garden in their own allotments (Greenhalgh and Worpole, 1995).

Young people in parks and other green spaces tend to cause concern amongst adult users and indeed their actions do sometimes cause damage. The common reaction amongst parks managers is to regard young people with suspicion and see them as a nuisance. Young people's use of parks could be better managed so that it does not cause problems for others. For example, if they tend to use children's play areas inappropriately, leaving rubbish and graffiti, cleaning schedules can be altered to make sure these areas are cleaned and routine maintenance carried out in the mornings before parents with young children start to arrive. (Greenhalgh and Worpole, 1995)

Residential streets

As already discussed, children and young people are more likely to play in the streets near their homes than anywhere else. Some streets such as short cul-de-sacs, where car traffic tends to be very light and slow-moving, may be seen by parents and children as reasonably suitable for play. The development of home zones – play-friendly residential street designs – shows that streets can successfully meet the needs of children as well as drivers (Biddulph, 2001). Other research also shows how street design and layout can promote play and allow children to move around on their own. Housing developments that offer children the best opportunities for playing in the streets near their homes are those with the greatest variety of places and the slowest traffic (Wheway and Millward,1997).

Traffic calming measures in residential areas go part way to opening up the streets for children's play but developments such as home zones provide more comprehensive measures that attempt to cater for the outdoor space needs of all the residents in the area.

> ### Cavell Way Home Zone, Sittingbourne, Swale: redesigning residential streets for play
>
> Cavell Way in Sittingbourne, Swale is one of nine national home zone pilots – residential streets where the car is a guest and other uses of the street space such as play are positively encouraged.
>
> Children in Cavell Way already use the street for a wide range of play activities. As part of the home zone project, Moat House Housing Society had semi-permanent play markings installed on the road. The aim was to offer children another resource for their play and also to signal to drivers that children are around.

Playing on the street at Cavell Way

The children were involved in choosing the designs that were painted quickly and efficiently by a firm that usually designs school playgrounds. The four patterns cost around £200 and will last for about a year. The lack of permanence is an advantage as new designs can be chosen each time it is renewed.

The markings are situated in a 'hammer head' turning at the end of a cul-de-sac so there is no danger of through traffic. Replicating this idea on public roads would be difficult, but the idea can be used on private roads or parking courts.

Other open spaces

The sorts of places children want to play in and which are attractive to them include flowing terrain where they can wonder and move about and do their own thing. It is important that the pedestrian and cycle networks are available to them and that they can find opportunities to play within these routes. Interesting and varied surfaces and topography also provide interesting places for children to play (Moore, 1990).

Developing the natural environment as a play space for children can be both cost effective and rewarding. 'Children need "wild space". A space "not made by people" has an essential quality for children – they feel free to be there, to manipulate it and to impose "ownership" on it. If this is not available we may need to create and maintain such a space, keeping our intervention to a minimum.' (Wood, 2001)

Well kept 'greenways' also provide a natural environment where children can play. These are open spaces or natural areas that are linear in form. They can be established along natural corridors including steams, rivers or ridges, or can follow along man-made routes such as canals, disused railways or rights of way. They provide a natural or landscaped passage or route for pedestrians or cyclists and can serve as linking routes between parks and other green spaces, natural areas and residential areas. They are also useful for recreational pursuits such as jogging, walking and roller-blading. For children they offer many opportunities for play (Godfrey, 1997).

The ideal housing development would be designed so that children could move freely through the neighbourhood, enjoy a wide variety of social interactions and opportunities for physical, imaginative and creative play. Wheway and Millard offer a set of measurable objectives for architects, planners, estate managers and others on how children's needs might be met in residential areas (Wheway and Millward, 1997).

Much of this guide focuses on the practical challenge of creating and improving outdoor play spaces and opportunities for children and young people. But this practical work takes place in a context shaped in part by policies, strategies and initiatives at national and local level. This concluding chapter takes some of the concerns raised in the rest of the guide – planning strategically for local needs, involving children and young people, encouraging good practice in design – and links them to some key emerging policy debates.

Strategy and policy

In recent years central government and local authorities have begun to recognise the value and importance of parks and other green spaces, play spaces and other recreational space. In 2001 the Government set up an Urban Green Spaces Taskforce to advise on 'proposals for improving the quality of our urban parks, play areas and green spaces' (DTLR, 2001b). The Taskforce report, the Government's response to it and the revised PPG 17 (DTLR, 2002), all to be published during 2002, will be key documents in setting the policy and planning framework for play spaces.

Alongside this, the Government's Planning Green Paper (DTLR, 2001c) proposes that much of the present development plan system is to be replaced by a Local Development Framework, which will 'connect up with the Local Community Strategy'. Community strategies are themselves a statutory requirement of the Local Government Act 2000 to 'promote the economic, social and environmental well-being of their areas and contribute to the achievement of sustainable development'. This gives much scope for the promotion of cultural and recreational provision such as parks and children's play.

At the same time, there is growing interest in children's and young people's play, leisure and free time. At national level this is evident, for instance, in the work of the Government's Children and Young People's Unit (CYPU). The CYPU is developing a strategy covering all services for children and young people, which explicitly embraces free-time and leisure (CYPU, 2001b). It has also drawn up core principles for children's involvement in the planning, delivery and evaluation of government policies and services (CYPU, 2001a). These principles support one of the main arguments running through this guide: the importance of involving children and young people in shaping their built environment.

Another key theme of this guide is the need for local play space development to be tackled strategically rather than in a piecemeal fashion. In many local authorities, quantitative spatial standards, often based on the six-acre standard (NPFA,

2001), which addresses qualitative and quantitative issues, are used to try to achieve this. There are widely differing views on the usefulness of standards. NPFA gives a useful overview of the advantages and disadvantages of standards in general.

The advantages and disadvantages of standards

There is an ongoing debate about the usefulness of quantitative spatial standards in the light of their advantages and disadvantages. It is likely that standards of the right form could play a part in planning and protecting play space. But more work is needed to explore the use and effectiveness of existing standards, in order to see how useful they are as a mechanism for improving play opportunities for children at the local level.

Advantages of standards
- provide a starting point for determining levels of provision;
- easy for planners, politicians and the public to understand;
- set clear targets for space that allow comparisons and measure improvement;
- can improve quality;
- can help to protect spaces from development threats;
- can support equitable allocation of funding and resources;
- support provision of play space in new developments.

Disadvantages of standards
- may discourage creativity;
- may have a weak theoretical basis;
- may be inflexible and unable to take account of local circumstances;
- application is difficult in areas where land uses are largely fixed;
- may be applied automatically without checking against local needs or wishes;
- may work against local participation;
- can be difficult to capture some important factors (such as location);
- may take little account of quality;
- it may be unclear whether there is a minimum, desirable or optimum standard.

Source: adapted from NPFA, 2001

Research

Writing this guide has highlighted that, though there is useful published data on children's activities in the outdoors as a whole, there is a lack of empirical research into dedicated play space (with the exception of the safety of equipment and surfacing). We know little about levels or patterns of use, the supply and distribution of dedicated spaces, the benefits to children and the overall picture about quality. There is also little information about how children use and value 'neglected space' for their play. Research into these issues will help to ensure that public funding is being well spent.

Supporting good practice

Most play spaces are managed by adults whose main interests and skills rarely include expertise in children's play. The adults who have play expertise – playworkers, some landscape architects and others – tend to have little input into the design of unsupervised spaces such as play areas and playgrounds. If playworkers, children and play spaces managers worked more closely together, many more children could reap the benefits of the expertise of playworkers. Given this, it may be helpful to examine the training, qualification and experience appropriate for those responsible for play spaces.

More broadly, there is no dedicated national focus for sharing and developing best practice in creating and designing dedicated play spaces. In other issues, bodies such as Learning through Landscape and the National Federation of City Farms and Community Gardens play a crucial role in supporting local projects and improving quality, through networking, training, information and sharing and developing standards. The need for a similar body or focus for outdoor play is all the more clear given the wide variation in the provision of outdoor play space in different local authorities (Cole-Hamilton and Gill, 2002).

Funding

During the 1980s and 1990s cuts in public spending at the local level, and the move to competitive tendering of many local services, led to reductions in spending on parks, playgrounds and other outdoor spaces. More recently, the introduction of new funding streams from central government and the National Lottery is improving the economic picture, but also making it more complex.

The New Opportunities Fund (NOF) has played, and will continue to play, a key role. Its £125 million 'Green Spaces, Sustainable Communities' initiative includes several programmes that aim to improve the quality and/or use of outdoor space. One of these, Better Play (a partnership between Barnardo's and the Children's Play Council) has an explicit focus on play, though its funding is almost exclusively for revenue projects. Plans are in hand for a much larger £200 million NOF programme on play, which should support capital projects.

While this new funding is welcome it has created two major problems. The tendency to target areas based, for example, on disadvantage, can make it difficult for local authorities to plan their spending, leading to support for some areas while others are left out. In addition, targeted initiatives and the National Lottery both provide funding for only a fixed period.

This can leave providers without the money to ensure that play space is sustained, maintained and developed over the long term. This situation is not limited to play space, but its resolution is all the more critical given the long life that play spaces are expected to have.

For many local children and young people and their families, play spaces are a vital, valued and daily part of the built environment. This guide aims to help local people come together to make them exciting and attractive places to play. But it also aims to stimulate some radical new thinking at all levels about how neighbourhoods as a whole can become more friendly and fun for children and young people.

Audit Commission (1994) *The Quality Exchange Leisure Services: Playgrounds and play areas*

Biddulph, M (2001) *Home Zones: A planning and design guide.* Policy Press

Child Accident Prevention Trust (2001) *Safe Kids Campaign: parents and children's poll.* Child Accident Prevention Trust

Children's Play Council and The Children's Society (2001) Press release for Playday. The Children's Society

Children's Play Council, Kidsactive and Mencap (2002) *Parliamentary Briefing: Children with Disabilities (Play Areas) Bill.* Mencap

Cole-Hamilton, I and Gill, T (2002) *Making the Case for Play: Building strategies and policies for school aged children.* National Children's Bureau

Cole-Hamilton, I, Harrop, A and Street, C (2002) *Making the Case for Play: Gathering the evidence.* National Children's Bureau

CYPU (2001a) *Learning to Listen: Core principles for the involvement of children and young people.* Children and Young People's Unit

CYPU (2001b) *Building a Strategy for Children and Young People: Consultation document.* Children and Young People's Unit

Davies, R and Heseltine, P (2000) *A Guide to the European Playground Equipment and Surfacing Standards.* RoSPA

DCMS (2000) *Creating opportunities: Guidance for local authorities in England on local cultural strategies.* Department for Culture, Media and Sport

Dekeyser, P (1999) Children's participation: needs and wants as a means to creating better play environments, *PlayRights*, 20, 2/3, 6-7

DoE (1973), *Children at Play.* Department of the Environment

DETR (2000a) *Planning Policy Guidance Note No. 3: Housing.* Department of the Environment, Transport and the Regions (now Department for Transport, Local Government and the Regions)

DETR (2000b) *Preparing Community Strategies: Government guidance to local authorities.* Department of the Environment, Transport and Regions (now Department for Transport, Local Government and Regions)

DTLR (2001a) *Road Accidents Great Britain: 2000.* Department for Transport, Local Government and the Regions (Table 28a)

DTLR (2001b) *Green Spaces, Better Places: Interim report of the Urban Green Spaces Taskforce.* Department for Transport, Local Government and the Regions

DTLR (2001c) *Planning: Delivering a fundamental change.* Department for Transport, Local Government and the Regions

DTLR (2001d) *Planning Obligations: Delivering a Fundamental Change.* Department for Transport, Local Government and the Regions

DTLR (2002) *Policy Planning Guidance Note No.17: Sport and Recreation.* Department for Transport, Local Government and the Regions

Families for Freedom (1997) *The Kids are Alright! Families for Freedom Child Safety Bulletins.* Families for Freedom

Freeman, C, Henderson, P and Kettle, J (1999) *Planning with children for better communities: The challenge to professionals.* Community Development Foundation, The Policy Press

Godfrey, J (1997) The value of greenways in children's play and education, *Playrights*, 19, 2, 19–26

Greenhalgh, L and Worpole, K (1995) *Park Life: Urban parks and social renewal*, A Report by Comedia in association with Demos, Comedia

Hampshire, R and Wilkinson, M (1999) *Youth Shelters and Sports Systems: A good practice guide.* Thames Valley Police

Hart, C H ed. (1993) *Children on Playgrounds: Research perspectives and applications.* State University of New York Press, New York

Hendricks, B (2001) *Designing for Play.* Ashgate Publishing Ltd

Heseltine, P (1985) *Play and Playgrounds in Rotterdam: A research approach.* Playboard, Association for Children's Play and Recreation Ltd

Heseltine, P (1998) *Assessing Risk on Children's Playground.* RoSPA

Heseltine, P (2000) *The Children's Playground: A basic guide.* RoSPA

Hicks, J (2000) *The Disability Discrimination Act 1995, Access to Public Play Space: A guide to audit.* Warwickshire County Playing Fields Association

Hughes, B (1994) *Lost childhoods: the case for children's play – the future of urban parks and open spaces.* Working Paper No.3, Comedia in association with Demos

Hughes, B (1996a) *Play Environments: A question of quality*, PLAYLINK

Hughes, B (1996b) *A Playworker's Taxonomy of Play Types*, PLAYLINK (new edition due 2002)

Humberside Playing Fields Association (1982) *Talking about play: A survey of the view of rural children.* Humberside Playing Fields Association

References

Huttenmoser, M and Degen-Zimmerman, D (1995) *Lebensräume für Kinder*, Maria Meierhofer-Institut für das Kind, Zürich (Summarised English Translation available from CPIS)

Matthews, H (2001) *Children and Community Regeneration: Creating better neighbourhoods*. Save the Children

Matthews, H, Limb, M and Taylor, M (1998) *Reclaiming the street: The discourse of curfew*, Monograph 6. Centre for Children and Youth, University College Northampton

Melville, S (1998) *PLAYLINK Guidance on Play Policies*. Working Paper, PLAYLINK

de Monchaux, S (1981) *Planning with children in mind: A notebook for local planners and policy makers on children in the city environment*. New South Wales Department of Environment and Planning, Sydney

Moore, R C (1990) *Childhood's Domain: Play and place in child development*. MIG Communications, Berkeley, California

Morrow, V (2001) *Networks and neighbourhoods: children's and young people's perspectives*. Health Development Agency

National Playing Fields Association (1998) *Teenage Fun and Fitness*. Information Sheet No.15, National Playing Fields Association

National Playing Fields Association (2001) *The Six Acre Standard: Minimum standards for outdoor playing space*. National Playing Fields Association

National Playing Fields Association, Children's Play Council and PLAYLINK (2000) *Best Play: What play provision should do for children*. National Playing Fields Association (available from Children's Play Council)

New Economics Foundation (2001) *Prove it! Measuring impacts of renewal: Findings and recommendations*. Groundwork UK

O'Brien, M, Rustin, M and Greenfield, J (2000) *Childhood Urban Space and Citizenship: Child-sensitive urban regeneration*. University of North London

Parkinson C E (1985) *Where children play: an analysis of interviews about where children aged 5–14 normally play and their preferences for out-of-school activities*. Play Board

PLAYLINK (2002) *Play as Culture*. PLAYLINK

Play Safety Forum (2002) *Managing Risks in Play Provision: A position statement*. Children's Play Council

POD (1991) *POD's Ideas for Playgrounds* (2nd ed). Playgrounds on Demand, Perth, Australia (available from CPIS)

Sexty, C (2000) *Playing Out: Improving child safety in parks and open spaces*. NSPCC and ILAM (Institute of Leisure and Amenity Management)

References

Scott, R (2000) *Side by Side: guidelines for inclusive play*. Kidsactive

Stine, S (1997) *Landscapes for learning*. John Wiley & Sons Inc, New York

Tovell, D (2000) *Child's Play: a short history of the village of Parkeston, some childhood recollections and a discussion about the disappearance of a culture of play*. CPIS.

Valentine, G (1997) A safe place to grow up? Parenting, perceptions of children's safety and the rural idyll, *Journal of Rural Studies*, 13, 2, 137–148

Wheway, R and Millward, A (1997) *Child's Play: Facilitating play on housing estates*. Chartered Institute of Housing

Whyte, W (1980) The Social Life of Small, Urban Spaces. The Conservation Foundation, Washington DC

Wood, P (2001) *Growing Spaces for Play: The value of play in the natural environment*. Devon Play Association and RoSPA

Reference copies are available at the Children's Play Information Service.

Burns, D and Taylor, M (2000) *Auditing community participation: An assessment handbook.* Joseph Rowntree Foundation, The Policy Press

Brett, A, Moore, R and Provenzo, E (1993) *The complete playground book*, Syracuse University Press, Syracuse New York

Coffin, G and Morris, W (1989) *Children's outdoor play in the built environment: A handbook for all who design, plan or manage residential neighbourhoods.* National Children's Play and Recreation Unit (available from CPIS)

Freeman, C, Henderson P and Kettle, J (1999) *Planning with children for better communities: The challenge to professionals.* Community Development Foundation, The Policy Press

Hendricks, B (2001) *Designing for Play.* Ashgate Publishing Ltd

Matthews, H (2001) *Children and Community Regeneration: Creating better neighbourhoods.* Save the Children

Moore, R C (1990) *Childhood's Domain: Play and place in child's development.* MIG Communications, Berkeley, California

Moore, R C, Goltsman, S and Iacofano, D *eds.* (1992) *Play for all guidelines: Planning, design and management of outdoor play settings for all children*, MIG Communications. Berkeley California

National Playing Fields Association, Children's Play Council and PLAYLINK (2000) *Best Play: What play provision should do for children.* National Playing Fields Association (available from Children's Play Council)

Price, R and Stoneham, J (2001) *Making Connections: A guide to accessible greenspace.* The Sensory Trust, Eden Project

Scott, R (2000) *Side by Side: Guidelines for inclusive play.* Kidsactive

Sender, M (1992) *Design of children's play environments.* McGraw-Hill Inc, New York

Stine, S (1997) *Landscapes for learning.* John Wiley & Sons Inc, New York

Wheway, R and Millward, A (1997) *Child's Play: Facilitating play on housing estates.* Chartered Institute of Housing

Wood, P (2001) *Growing Spaces for Play: The value of play in the natural environment.* Devon Play Association and RoSPA

Children play in many different ways, and need facilities and resources that will enable them to do this. The following 15 play types and explanations are adapted from those given in *Best Play* (NPFA and others, 2000) and in Hughes, 1996b.

Communication play

Play using words, nuances or gestures. **Example:** mime, jokes, play acting, singing, debate, poetry.

Creative play

Play that allows a new response, the transformation of information or the awareness of new connections, with an element of surprise. **Example:** enjoying making something with a range of materials and tools for its own sake.

Deep play

Play that allows the child to encounter risky or even potentially life-threatening experiences, to develop survival skills and conquer fear. **Example:** leaping on to an aerial runway, riding a bike on a parapet, balancing on a high beam.

Dramatic play

Play that dramatises events in which the child is not a direct participator. **Example:** presentation of a TV show, an event on the street, a religious or festive event, even a funeral.

Exploratory play

Play to access factual information consisting of manipulative behaviours such as handling, throwing, banging or mouthing objects. **Example:** engaging with an object or area and, either by manipulation or movement, assessing its properties, possibilities and content, such as stacking bricks.

Fantasy play

Play that rearranges the world in the child's way, a way which is unlikely to occur. **Example:** playing at being a pilot flying around the world or the owner of an expensive car.

Imaginative play

Play where conventional rules that govern the physical world do not apply. **Example:** imagining you are, or pretending to be, a tree or ship, or patting a dog that isn't there.

Locomotor play

Movement in any and every direction for its own sake. **Example:** chase, tag, hide-and-seek, tree climbing.

Mastery play

Control of the physical and affective ingredients of the environments. **Example:** digging holes, changing the course of streams, constructing shelters, building fires.

Object play

Play that uses infinite and interesting sequences of hand–eye manipulations and movements. **Example:** examination and novel use of any object such as a cloth, paintbrush, cup.

Role play

Play exploring ways of being, although not normally of an intense personal, social, domestic or interpersonal nature. **Example:** brushing with a broom, dialling with a telephone, driving a car.

Rough and tumble play

Close encounter play that has less to do with fighting and more to do with touching, tickling, gauging relative strength, discovering physical flexibility and the exhilaration of display. **Example:** playful fighting, wrestling and chasing where children are obviously unhurt and giving every indication that they are enjoying themselves.

Social play

Play during which the rules and criteria for social engagement and interaction can be revealed, explored and amended. **Example:** any social or interactive situation that contains an expectation on all parties to abide by the rules or protocols such as games, conversations, making something together.

Socio-dramatic play

The enactment of real and potential experiences of an intense personal, social, domestic or interpersonal nature. **Example:** playing at house, going to the shops, being mothers and fathers, organising a meal or even having an argument.

Symbolic play

Play that allows control, gradual exploration and increased understanding, without the risk of being incomprehensible. **Example:** using a piece of wood to symbolise a person, or a piece of string to symbolise a wedding ring.

Bath and North East Somerset
Michael Follett
Play Development Officer
Education Service
PO Box 25, Riverside
Temple Street, Keynsham
Bristol BS31 1DN
Tel: 01225 395137
Fax: 01225 395147
Email: michael_follett@bathnes.gov.uk

Birmingham Groundwork
Amy Robertson
Project Manager (Landscape)
Groundwork Birmingham
65 Villa Road
Handsworth
Birmingham B19

Bognor Fun Bus
35 Lyon Street
Bognor Regis
PO21 1BW
Tel: 01243 869922

Bradford
Amenities and Landscape
Arts, Heritage and Leisure
1st floor
Jacob's Well
Bradford
BD1 5RW
Tel: 01274 752 648

Cambridge
Liz Mantle
The Children's Team
Community Development
Mandela House
4 Regent Street
Cambridge
CB21 1BY
Tel: 01223 457927
Email: Elizabeth.mantle@cambridge.gov.uk

Cavell Way
Caroline Field
Moat Housing Society
96 High Street
Sevenoaks
Kent
Email: carolinefield@moat.co.uk

Cuxton Teenage Village, Rochester
Peter Curran
Parish Clerk
296 The Tideway
Rochester
Kent ME1 3PS
Tel: 01634 846734

Devon@Play
Devon Play Association
Philippa Wood
15 Tweenaways
Buckfastleigh
Email: team@devonplay.co.uk
Website: www.devonplay.co.uk

Ealing
Jeff Parkinson
Play Service Manager
London Borough of Ealing
Percival House
14/16 Uxbridge Road
London
W5 2HL
Tel: 020 8758 5745
Email: JPARKIN@EALING.GOV.UK

Gloucester Play Space Audit
Pippa Levett
Neighbourhood Children's Commission
c/o Gloucestershire Neighbourhood Projects
Network
City Works
Alfred Street
Gloucester
GL1 4DF
Email: pip.levett@potts9.demon.co.uk

Heeley City Farm
Richards Road
Sheffield S2 3DT
Tel: 0114 258 0482
Email: farm@heeleyfarm.org.uk

Contacts for information on case studies

Kingston-upon-Hull
Helen Anglum
Humber and Wolds Community Council
14, Market Place
Howden
DN14 7BJ
Tel: 01430 430904

Lambeth
Department of Lifelong Learning
International House
Canterbury Crescent
London SW9 7QE
Tel: 020 7926 9561/3
email: pmcnally@lambeth.gov.uk

Leeds's Children's Fund
191-193 Chapel Town Road
Chapel Town
Leeds LS7 3DU
Tel: 0113 2626362
Email: leedschildrensfund@barnardos.org.uk

Leicester
Adrian Edge
Leicester City Council
Arts & Leisure Department
New Walk Centre
Welford Place
Leicester LE1 6ZG
Tel: 0116 252 7324
Fax: 0116 254 0590
Email: edgea001@leicester.gov.uk

Macclesfield & Vale Royal Groundwork
Peter Heberlet
Groundwork Macclesfield & Vale Royal
Adelphi Mill Gate Lodge
Grimshaw Lane
Bollington
Macclesfield
SK10 5JP
Email: macc.vr@groundwork.org.uk

Manchester Adventure Playgrounds
Tim Ferguson
Director
Unit 30
Greenhep Business Centre
Pencroft Way
Manchester
M15 6SS
Tel: 0161 226 0811
Web: www.manchesterplay.org.uk
Email: info@manchesterplay.org.uk

North Hull Adventure Playground
The Staff and Committee
Adventure Zone
Rear of University of Lincolnshire
Cottingham Road
Hull
HU6 7RT
Tel: 01482 492648
Fax: 01482 442497
Email: addy@the-adventure-zone.fsnet.co.uk

Northumberland Park, Haringey
Simon Rix or Sarah Hall-Craggs
Haringey Play Association
Unit 22F, N17 Studios
788 Tottenham High Road
London N17
Email: simon.rix@btinternet.com or
sarahharpa@btinternet.com

Nuneaton and Bedworth
Simon D Jones
Sport and Community Development Officer
Nuneaton and Bedworth Borough Council
Leisure Services
Council House
Coton Road
Nuneaton
Warwickshire
CV11 5AA
Visit the website where various contact details
can be easily found
www.nuneatonandbedworthskateparks.com

Oxfordshire Youth Shelters
R Hampshire
CPDA
Thames Valley Police
Welch Way
Witney
Oxfordshire
OX8 7HN

Sheffield
Ian Mitchell
Parks, Woodlands and Countryside
Meersbrook Park
Brook Road
Sheffield
S8 9FL

Shoreditch
Michael Hammond
Project Coordinator
Shoreditch our way
27 Provost Street
London
N1 7NH
Tel: 020 7324 5595
Fax: 020 7253 5778
Email: m.hammond@shoreditchourway.org.uk
Report available entitled 'Adults will never listen'

South Somerset
Tim Huxley
Sport & Leisure Officer
South Somerset District Council
Old Kelways
Somerton Road
Langport
TA10 9YE
Tel: 01458 257437
Email: tim.huxley@southsomerset.gov.uk
For information about BMX play tracks look at:
www.jenks44.fsbusiness.co.uk

Little Dorrit Park, Southwark
Adele Morris
Bankside Open Spaces Trust
5 King James Street
London
SE1 0RU
Tel: 020 7261 1009
Email: adele@bost.org.uk

Stamshaw Adventure Playground, Portsmouth
Tim Head
Stamshaw Adventure Playground
Western Terrace
Portsmouth
PO2 8JX

Tribe Enterprises
Andrew Southwood
Tribe Enterprises Ltd
Unit 16
Rivers Business Centre
Victoria Street
High Wycombe
HP1 2LT
Tel: 08451 300777
Web: www.tribeskate.com

Walsall
Walsall Metropolitan Borough Council
Keith Rimmer
Play Areas Manager
Leisure and Community services
Civil Centre
Darwall Street
Walsall
WS1 1TZ
Tel/fax: 01922 724065

Action for Leisure
c/o Warwickshire College
Moreton Morrell Centre
Moreton Morrell
Warwickshire
CV35 9BL
Tel: 01926 650195

Centre for Accessible Environments
Nutmeg House
60 Gainsford Street
London
SE1 2NY
Tel: 020 7357 8182

Child Accident Prevention Trust
4th floor Clerks Court
18-20 Farringdon Lane
London
EC1R 3AU
Tel: 020 7608 3828

Children's Play Council
c/o National Children's Bureau
8 Wakley Street
London EC1V 7QE
Tel: 020 7843 6016

Children's Play Information Service
National Children's Bureau
8 Wakley Street
London EC1V 7QE
Tel: 020 7843 6303

Federation of City Farms and Community Gardens
The Green House
Hereford Street
Bristol
BS3 4NA
Tel: 0117 923 1800

Groundwork UK
85-87 Cornwall Street
Birmingham
BN3 3BY
Tel: 0121 236 8565

Institute of Leisure & Amenity Management
Ilam House
Lower Basildon
Reading
RG8 9NE
Tel: 01491 874800

Kidsactive
Pryor's Bank
Bishop's Park
London
SW6 3LA
Tel: 020 7731 1435

Learning Through Landscapes
3rd Floor, Southside Offices
The Law Courts
Winchester
SO23 9DL
Tel: 01962 846258

National Children's Bureau
8 Wakley Street
London
EC1V 7QE
Tel: 020 7843 6000

National Playbus Association
93 Whitby Road
Bristol
BS4 3QF
Tel: 0117 977 5375

National Playing Fields Association
Stanley House
St Chads Place
London
WC1X 9HH
Tel: 020 7833 5360

National Society for the Prevention of Cruelty to Children
42 Curtain Road
London
EC2A 3NH
Tel: 020 7825 2500

PLAYLINK
The Co-op Centre
Unit 5 Upper
11 Mowll Street
London
SW9 6BG
Tel: 020 7820 3800

RoSPA
Edgbaston Park
353 Bristol Road
Birmingham
B5 7ST
Tel: 0121 248 2000

The Sensory Trust
c/o Eden Project
Watering Lane Nursery
Pentewan
St Austell
Cornwall
PL26 6B